HappyHour
GUIDEBOOK

2016 EDITION

Portland Happy Hour Guidebook
Tenth Edition ©2016 Half-Full Enterprises
All rights reserved.
No portion of this book may be reproduced in any form without previous written permission from the publisher.

ISBN: 978-0-9909029-1-1

Self-published with all content including research, reviews, illustrations, cover, maps, and design by Cindy Anderson

<u>Credits:</u>
Editing by Mary Beth Saddoris (writebrainediting@gmail.com)
Locally printed in the U.S. by Journal Graphics; Portland, OR
Call Carol Kersley, Sales Associate 503-358-8341

Due to the fluid nature of the ever-changing Portland Happy Hour scene, Half-Full Enterprises cannot accept responsibility for any complications that may arise from using the information in this book. Every effort has been made to maintain accuracy, but things change, and Half-Full Enterprises cannot guarantee that the information in this book is or will be accurate. The opinions expressed in this book are just that, opinions of the author. The author did not receive any endorsement earnings (or bribes!) from any bar/restaurant/tavern in the writing of this book. Finally, you are responsible for your own actions, before, during and after using the information provided in this book. Drink responsibly! Half-Full Enterprises is not liable for any irresponsible actions on your part, including but not limited to drunk dialing, hooking up with an ex-boyfriend or girlfriend, hurting yourself or hurting someone else.

Half-Full Enterprises / Cindy Anderson
250 NE Tomahawk Island Drive #D17; Portland, OR 97217
Website www.happyhourguidebook.com
Facebook www.facebook.com/HappyHourGuidebook
Twitter twitter.com/PDXHappyHour
Email pdxinfo@happyhourguidebook.com

Contents

Celebrating 10 Years!
A Retrospective, Memory Lane,
About the New Format 5

Notes/Tipsys/About Reviews . . . 8

Maps 13
Downtown
NW/Pearl | NW/Nob Hill
NE/Mississippi Area | NE/Lloyd Center
NE/Alberta | NE/Fremont
SE and Central Eastside | Waterfront

Gold Medal Superstars 23

"Golden Tickets" (64 Coupons) . . 49

Reviews 119

Your Turn 251

Make new friends, but keep the old..

One is silver and the other is gold.

Celebrating 10 Years!
A RETROSPECTIVE

Wow! Little did I know what I was getting into back in 2006, when I thought I might write this little guide to Happy Hours. What a wild ride it has been, and how exciting to see it all change so much! There are now SO many more restaurants than I'd ever thought this city could hold, and for good or bad, more growth is on its way…

The expansion we've experienced in Happy Hour Land is crazy! My first edition had just 100 places in it, and was very all-encompassing at the time. My last edition covered more than 600 places, and the book was so thick, it could physically stand up on its own!

Over the years, I've also perfected my format, yet I've always kept the fast-find formula that makes it easy to find the perfect spot for Happy Hour, whether you're with a friend or on your own.

I've seen them come, and I've watched them go. Sometimes at a great and sad surprise, and sometimes understandably. Sometimes in less than one year! It's a tough business.

My final wise words? Go forth and intrepidly chase down new favorites, but never neglect your classic, old stand-bys. They are silver and gold :-)

Memory Lane
BLASTS FROM THE PAST

In writing this 10th Anniversary edition, I often referred back to my first "baby" – the original 2007 Happy Hour Guidebook (#1). It was so fun to remember all of the old favorites that are now gone! I invite you to take a minute and reminisce alone or with a friend. It's fun to think about all of the good times, and actually a great exercise for the brain, too.

From the 2007 Edition	**Some Others We Miss**
Alessandro's	50 Plates
Aura	Bay 13
Barcode	Belly
Betty Ford	Brasserie Montmarte
The City	Carafe
The Empire Room	Carlyle
Fernando's Hideaway	Fenouil
Greek Cusina	Gilt Club
Green Papaya	Fratelli
H20	Limo Peruvian
Imbibe	The Maiden
Kincaid's	Metrovino
Lucy's Table	Portland Steak & Chophouse
McFadden's	Ten 01
Olea	Typhoon
Perry's	Vindalho
Rose & Raindrop	Virgo & Pisces
Roux	Wildwood
Voluer	Wine Down on 28th
Voodoo Lounge	

About the New Format

SHAKING IT UP FOR YEAR #10

The Size
The book had grown too big! Places were getting lost in the shuffle, and we were all losing focus. It was a whopping 432 pages, and had become unruly. I went back to the basics, making this a real *guide*, like if I could have a long Happy Hour conversation with you, these are the places I'd make sure you knew about.

The Pages
This book is really pretty! Because it has less pages, I was able to use lots of color, as well as nicer paper. It's also more clear and user-friendly, with better direction. I dropped the "big number" ratings since I give every place in this version an overall 10 points, including all the newbies because I'm pulling for them to get there no matter where they are starting from this year.

The Maps
I kept *all* the restaurants and bars plotted on the maps, but highlighted the ones I've included reviews for in this book. That way, you can still see all of the options, and refer to last year's book if you want to read more. Don't have it? Order online at www.happyhourguidebook.com!

The Coupons
Woo-hoo! I've really loaded you up with coupons this year! Just remember to bring them with you and use them!

Notes & Disclaimers

Accuracy of information: Things change! Graciously accept this fluidity and adjust your attitude accordingly. As of this writing, the information herein is current. Every effort has been made to present information accurately. Check the website for updates.

Crowd scene: An element that can greatly vary. I elected not to try to qualify the type of person typically visiting a certain place, but rather encourage you to reserve judgement as well and be accepting and tolerant—and even friendly—to your fellow bar patrons. Also, please be aware that the more popular places get crowded. Be flexible, prompt, and patient. I hope this book will encourage you to get out there and explore! Every place in this book is worth checking out.

Service: I didn't comment on this aspect as "one bad apple doesn't spoil the whole bunch." Be aware that sometimes it's service via bartender only, and you'll have to order at the bar. If things are taking a while, be proactive, yet polite.

Tipping: Servers may have to make just as many trips for you as a regular diner. Please consider the effort—not the totally low bill—and be extra-generous for good service!

Rating and Judging: All judging is based on Happy Hour only. You may find you have different opinions of places. I called 'em as I saw 'em and in comparison to others. Take your own notes for future reference throughout the book. Record your adventures within and it can be a fun walk down Memory Lane!

Do not drink and drive (but of course).

Happy Hours are often relegated to bar area only. Mostly, I've commented on the restaurant atmosphere overall, including outdoor seating (which may not always be available to the Happy Hour crowd). Ask before you are seated to confirm available service.

Factoids & Tipsys

- Be sure to become a **facebook fan!** Get clued in to Happy Hour action and chime in with your opinions and experiences too. Win contests and get deals!

 Portland Happy Hour Guidebook

- Lots of places go all night ('til close) on Sunday or on another weeknight. Look for the ★s in this book to most easily find **extended hours.**

- Be aware of the Happy Hour **end-time** and pad your order by at least 10 minutes. Confirm with your waiter if you made it on time.

- Incorporate another **activity** such as a movie, concert, the Chinese Gardens, or a long walk into your night out.

- Not all places can accommodate larger **groups.** Call first. It's fun to organize a get-together!

- Sign up for the **email** list at your favorite restaurants. You'll be in the know about special events and offers. And maybe get a coupon here and there too.

- Live in gratitude—most cities do not have Happy Hours. I know—shocking! And we have the best.

- Things change! Please **report changes** you find to: pdxinfo@happyhourguidebook.com. Also, sign up for the monthly newsletter to be in-the-know.

- Check in with the **website** to keep up with changes!

www.happyhourguidebook.com

Keep smilin'!

Live happy!

☐ Step out of your comfort zone and discover a new place you've never tried before. Explore!

☐ Revisit a long-time, classic favorite.

☐ Hit at least three Happy Hours a month :-)

☐ Visit a friend in a different area of town. Try a couple places in a new neighborhood.

☐ Play tourist right here in Portland – and go to Happy Hour near your chosen site.

☐ Invite a new friend to meet for Happy Hour.

☐ Invite an old friend, or maybe two or three!

☐ Ask a networking contact to meet for a drink. Happy Hour can be much more fun than coffee.

☐ Make a monthly date night with your special someone. Or maybe make that weekly…

☐ Pick up "drinkercising" as a hobby – plan some exercise or walking along with that Happy Hour!

☐ Follow **"Portland Happy Hour Guidebook"** facebook page for all kinds of fun ideas!

Review Pages

Highlights weekend and/or Extended All-Night Happy Hours

Black stars indicate extended hours

★ = 7:00pm end time on the <u>maps</u>

Rated on a scale of 1-3

Just okay = **1**
Pretty Good = **2**
Great! = **3**

SAT / ALL SUN & MON

Lechon

Downtown (East)
113 SW Naito Pkwy
(503) 219-9000
www.lechonpdx.com

– 2016 –
TOP TEN
Superstar

New!

Happy Hours
3:00-6:00pm and 9:00pm-close Daily
(from 2:00pm Sat-Sun); ★All Night Sun-Mon

Food Deals 3 $3.00-$7.00
Love at first bite! Even before that as everything is plated beautifully! Lots to choose from with a talented, caring chef skillfully throwing down Argentinian and Chilean specialties like ceviche, empanadas, forest mushrooms, salad, stew, yuca chips, burgers, mussels, and *much* more.

Drink Specials 3
$4.00 beer; $5.00 wine; $4.00 wells
$6.00-$7.00 specialty cocktails

Atmosphere 3
Very cool space in an old, historic building across from the waterfront park just south of the Saturday Market. Stately, giant arched windows, exposed brick walls, and two huge fish and jellyfish tanks.

New this Year/First Impressions
Every once in a while, a place comes along and really knocks my socks off. Lechon is one of those places, and I am so excited about it!!!!

Mark up your books!

Fold down page corners!

Plan ahead! Make notes!

Map Information

Plus some scattered favorites in
Beaverton, Lake Oswego, Tigard, Vancouver

- ● Dots mark restaurant location
- ★ Stars indicate places that go until 7:00pm
- Highlighted restaurants are faves and reviewed

Downtown-West

Downtown-East

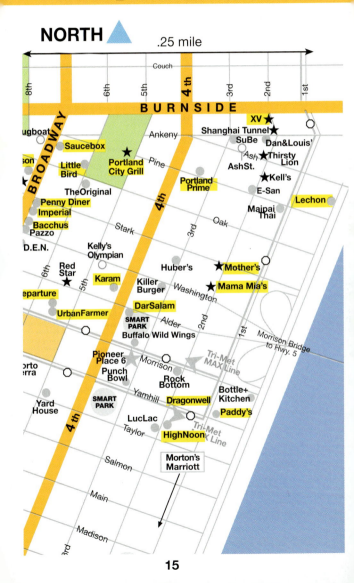

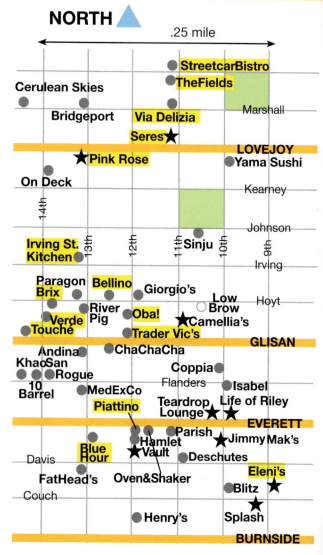

NW / Nob Hill

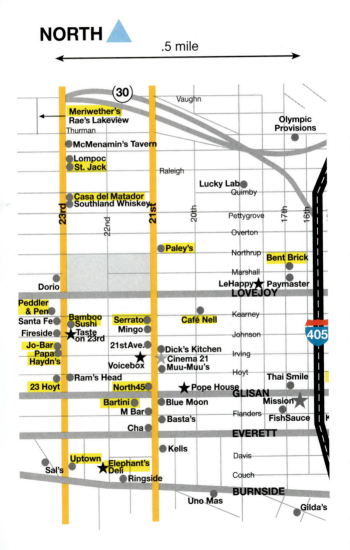

NE/Mississippi +

NE/Alberta & Fremont

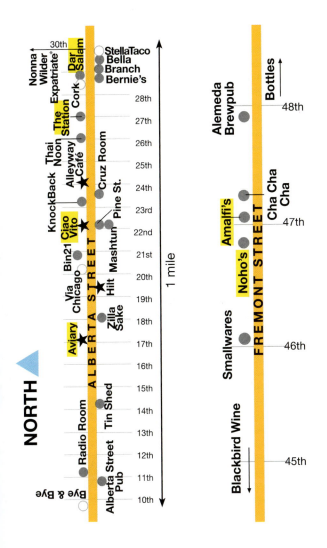

NE/Lloyd Center-ish

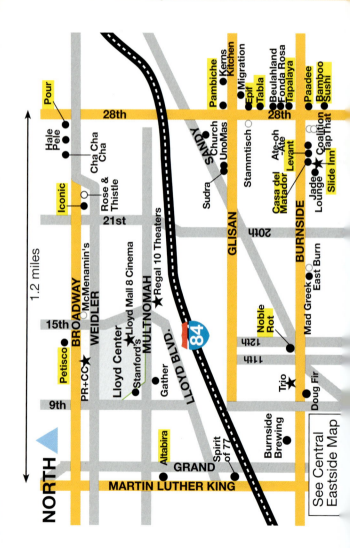

SE/Central Eastside

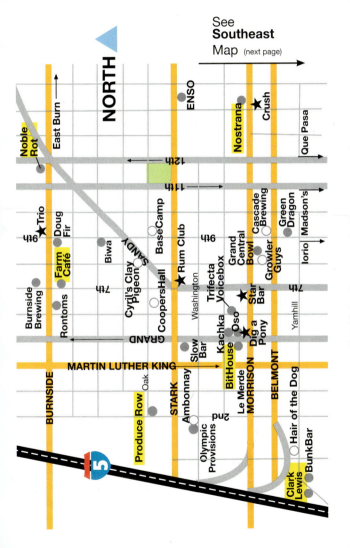

SE Maps

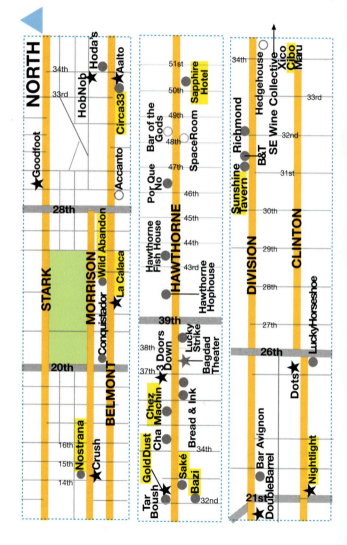

Gold Medal Superstars

As the reigning Happy Hour Queen, I'm frequently asked: "What's your favorite Happy Hour?" Tricky question, but here you go... My three favorite new places, places I go most often, a variety of food and ambiance, and *the* original!

~ 2016 ~
TOP 10
Superstar

Ruth's Chris
Mama Mia Trattoria
Seres Restaurant
Thirst Bistro
North 45
McCormick & Schmick's
Bellino
Lechon
Amalfi's
Altabira

GOLDEN FAVORITES

Playing Favorites...

Since I am so often asked what my favorite Happy Hours are, I figured I'd put some deep thought into it and come up with an answer. I could never pick just one, and picking 10 is nearly impossible, too! But these are the places I totally love and frequent, and I think capture a nice, wide variety in what's possible when a restaurant gives it their all...

Altabira
Yay! New to town in the summer of 2015, this place is a real stunner! Located on the rooftop of the Hotel Eastlund near the Convention Center, it hosts a wonderful outdoor patio with firepits and lounge areas, big local tap line-up, and excellent food.

Amalfi's
Everyone simply loves Amalfi's! It has a huge loyal customer following that spans generations, and a lovely outdoor patio. Romantic but fun, and in capable hands continually improving on perfection.

Bellino Trattoria Siciliana
A Sicilian newcomer this year, they impress on all fronts with decor, food, wines and service. I look forward to every taste, and know I'll treasure it. A low-key and understated "don't miss!"

Lechon
Totally a love-at-first-bite kind of place! I went back twice in one week when I first discovered it. Inside a cool historic building, they have fully capitalized on its unique charm and created a warm space that's open breakfast through late-evening drinks.

Mama Mia Trattoria
The official "Happy Hour of the Year" just last year, and they just keep getting better and better! They aim to please and really bend over backwards to achieve. Impressive and astounding!

McCormick & Schmick's
The rumor is that they are responsible for initiating Happy Hour as we know it in Portland! Verified or not, they are true pros. I'm from Chicago, where they did not have Happy Hour until a few months ago (true story), except for at McCormick & Schmick's.

North 45
In my opinion, this is Portland's best bar/gastropub/barstaurant! Fresh, clean, fun, social and pleasant. Plus the city's best mussels, tastiest pommes frites and 30 Belgian beers.

Ruth's Chris Steakhouse
All across the nation, people enjoy this fine-dining, elegant restaurant, and how nice of them to host such a great Happy Hour so we can go often!

Seres
They take Chinese food to a whole new level! And the menu is so extensive and deliciously perfect that even 10 years later, I am still amazed.

Thirst Bistro
With beautiful views of the Willamette River and eastern skyline, it doesn't get much better than Thirst on a sunny summer day. And with such superb wine and food, it's hard to beat, period!

American Cuisine

16 Local Craft Beer Taps ~ 50 Bottled Beers

Happy Hour Daily from 4 - 6 pm

Spacious Patio with Stunning City Views

Available for Private Parties

Altabira
CITY TAVERN

Top of the Hotel Eastlund

1021 NE Grand Avenue, 6th Floor
The Lloyd District of Portland's East Side
503.963.3600 | **altabira.com**

CHEF/OWNER DAVID MACHADO

Altabira

Situated on the top floor of the Hotel Eastlund, Altabira City Tavern is an American beer-centric restaurant and bar by Portland chef/restaurateur, David Machado (best known as the man behind Hotel Modera's Nel Centro, and former owner of Lauro Mediterranean Kitchen). The restaurant is perched high above Portland's fast-growing Lloyd District on the city's East Side. With sweeping views of downtown, Altabira City Tavern offers smart pairings of food and drink in a modern yet casual setting.

Altabira features 16 rotating taps of local craft beers, plus select European and Northwest wines and locally distilled spirits. The menu offers fresh, seasonal, American cuisine — creative dishes that showcase the flavor and variety of the selection of local craft beers. Altabira's dining room seats 50, the spacious rectangular bar seats 34. A gorgeous patio — with windbreaks, heaters and fire pits — accommodates 103. Five stunning private dining and meeting rooms — including the 3,400 square foot Cosmopolitan Grand Ballroom— feature floor to ceiling windows and breathtaking views.

Let Altabira help plan your next private event or meeting!

503-963-3603
events@altabira.com

Amalfi's
RESTAURANT & MERCATO est. 1959

MERCATO NOW OPEN!

An Italian-inspired marketplace specializing in fresh, house-made foods, local delicacies and Italian imported products. Grab-and-go pastas, salads, pizza... Dinner is done. Don't forget to grab a bottle of wine when you pick up your pizza!

TAKE AMALFI'S HOME WITH YOU!

 $5 MENTION THIS AD AND SAVE $5 ON YOUR PURCHASE OF $20 OR MORE

4703 NE Fremont   503.284.6747   AmalfisRestaurant.com

Amalfi's

Overview

Established in 1959, Amalfi's has become a staple gathering place in the Fremont neighborhood. Perfect for date nights, private events, "girl's night out" and family affairs, there's a little something for everyone here!

Try the award winning pizza, or perhaps classic Italian comfort-food is more your style. Want to liven things up? Happy Hour is offered both in the bar, and fireside on the outdoor piazza. Not to forget their hand-crafted cocktails, local rotating brews and ample wine.

¡Salud!

The Mercato at Amalfi's is now open!

This Italian-style marketplace is your new destination for a unique take-out experience. Stop in for "grab & go" house-made specialties, Italian-imported products and local delicacies. Choose from a variety of entrees, take & bake pizzas, salads, desserts....oh and....don't forget the vino!

For menus, catering, and private event information go to: www.amalfisrestaurant.com

503.284.6747

 BELLINO TRATTORIA SICILIANA

The heart of Sicily in the heart of the Pearl

1230 NW Hoyt · 503.208.2992 · bellinoportland.com

Bellino

Overview
Portland's only Sicilian restaurant, Bellino Trattoria Siciliana (Bellino) features authentic Sicilian, Italian cuisine and an extensive list of imported Italian wines.

Food
Classic dishes that are deeply rooted in Sicilian culture, using local and sustainable ingredients from the NW, including traditional meat, fish, and vegetarian dishes and freshly-prepared pasta dishes, with gluten-free options available. They also feature tapas, like Arancini and Crochette, which are popular street food in Sicily. Go for Brunch on the weekends or the Monday night Italian Supper Club, Festa Italiana, which celebrates cuisine from all over Italy, as well as dishes from the regular menu.

Chef/Owner
Born in Palermo, Sicily's capital city, Executive Chef Francesco Inguaggiato grew up learning the traditional preparation of Sicilian food while working with his mother in his grandfather's Trattoria in Palermo. Interestingly, he played professional basketball for the Italian League in Italy for 18 years. After moving to the U.S. in 2004 and opening two successful Italian restaurants in Texas, Inguaggiato brings the authentic food and culture of his homeland to Portland. With Bellino, which is Inguaggiato's mother's maiden name, Bellino Trattoria Siciliana has deep roots in family, heritage and history.

Lechon

LeChon is a South American dining experience that seamlessly combines the fiery cooking of Argentina, Chile, and Patagonia, with the creative inspiration of Chef Jaco Smith.

Located in a beautiful historic building in downtown Portland, LeChon is a great draw for locals and guests visiting the Portland area.

Enjoy live music every weekend with sprawling views of Tom McCall Waterfront Park. In addition to the main dining area, a private atrium space can accommodate up to 45 guests, making LeChon a destination for a variety of private dining events.

LeChon is open all day, seven days a week, with ample parking available.

Taste your way through the creative cocktail list at the bar in front of the impressive jellyfish tank or savor the flavors of South America with inventive tapas while overlooking the open kitchen. A family-style approach to LeChon's dining experience will have you feeling like part of "la familia" in no time.

For menus, catering, and private event information go to: www.lechonpdx.com

503.219.9000

Classic and Modern Italian Soul Food

The most extensive Italian menu in town!

You'll find timeless, traditional favorites like Chicken or Veal Parmigiana or our famous six-layers-tall Lasagna, served right alongside seasonal specials like Arancini Alla Bolognese or Calabrian Pork Sugo. Although we come from a long line of old-school Italian chefs, we are also experts in fresh and innovative NW cuisine.

Mama Mia
TRATTORIA

Call 503.295.6464 or visit
MAMAMIATRATTORIA.COM

439 SW 2ND AVE • DOWNTOWN PORTLAND • OREGON, 97204

Mama Mia Trattoria

Locally Owned and Family Operated

Beginning in 1904 and now in its 5th generation, the Mama Mia family continues to provide the absolutely most authentic, made-from-scratch Italian food, which has been enjoyed for generations in villages throughout both northern and southern Italy.

The menu consists of classic, creative, and contemporary Italian meals, with a focus on sustainability in sourcing the best local produce, and beef, chicken, and veal grown and raised here in the Pacific Northwest.

Mama Mia's location was built in 1886, and is easily visible at the intersection of SW Washington & 2nd Ave., just feet away from great shopping, the waterfront, mass transit & some of the most visited attractions in Downtown Portland. Three parking lots surround the building, as well as lots of street parking.

Mama Mia also showcases handcrafted cocktails, boutique Northwest and Italian beers, and an extensive list of both Pacific Northwest and Italian wines. All of this complements the soul of their modern and classic Italian cuisine.

For menus, catering, and private event information go to: www.mamamiatrattoria.com

(503) 295-6464

McCormick & Schmick's

History
Bill McCormick and Doug Schmick teamed up in the 1970s and went on to open 80 restaurants nationwide. McCormick & Schmick's Seafood Restaurants began with the purchase of Jake's Famous Crawfish located right here in Portland! The first-ever McCormick & Schmick's restaurant was opened here in 1979. In 2012, McCormick & Schmick's became a part of the Landry's, Inc. family, whose restaurants include local favorites Charthouse, Claim Jumper, The Heathman, Jake's Famous Crawfish, Jake's Grill, and Morton's. Author's Note: I've often heard that McCormick & Schmick's is credited for getting Happy Hour started in Portland, and everyone had to step up!

Food
Each restaurant's menu is printed twice daily, featuring the signature "Fresh List" highlighting an impressive number of fresh seafood varieties, in addition to aged steaks, poultry, entrée salads and pasta. McCormick & Schmick's commitment to local freshness is apparent in the seasonally inspired dishes and regionally inspired preparations offered. Not to mention the legendary Happy Hour.

McCormick & Schmick's Harborside
Located in the scenic RiverPlace Marina, with indoor and outdoor dining (a very enviable patio), and a spectacular view of the Willamette River. Portland's best lunchtime escape! Plus, stunning private and semi-private dining areas for corporate events or social gatherings.

North 45

Inspired by a love for international travel and its location on the 45th parallel, North 45 is a cozy NW 21st neighborhood pub serving craft beers, cocktails and favorite dishes from travels abroad (house specialty is mussels and frites), all made with local ingredients. They also offer a healthy selection of Belgian-style beer and 150+ bottles of the finest bourbons, ryes, Irish and Scotch whiskies around!

The concept was born while local owners were backpacking through South America in 2005. "We wanted to incorporate the intimacy and social elements of a pub, without labeling ourselves as an Irish or English pub. We figured a travel-themed pub is something that everybody can relate to."

North 45 has one of Portland's Best Patios, with outdoor seating available year-round. An 80-inch outdoor screen invites you to cheer on the Timbers, Trailblazers and futbol. Check out the annual Belgianfest event (taste 30+ Belgian style beers) or Brew Hog series, pairing ribs and local craft brewers on Thursdays from mid-October through mid-April.

Patrons are invited to share their travel stories and send postcards which hang on the walls.

North 45 is part of the IRC family (Independent Restaurant Concepts), which includes Circa 33, Paddy's, Produce Row Café, and The Station.

Ruth's Chris Steak House

Having just celebrated their 50th year in business in 2015, Ruth's Chris Steak House, which started out as a small corner restaurant in New Orleans, now has well over 100 locations throughout the world. Their upscale, luxury steak restaurants are known for their expertly prepared USDA Prime steaks served sizzling on a 500° plate, as well as their award-winning wine lists. Believing that the memory of a great meal stays with you long after the table's been cleared, Ruth's Chris Steak House is passionate about attention to detail and uses only the freshest and finest ingredients, including locally sourced produce.

The Portland location is just south of Pioneer Courthouse Square and mere steps from both the Arlene Schnitzer Concert Hall and the Portland Art Museum, making it a great destination for dinners before events, as well as for after-work gatherings, date nights, and special celebrations like anniversaries, birthdays and outings during the holiday season.

For menus, catering, and private event information go to: www.ruthschris.com/restaurant-locations/portland

(503) 221-4518

 **seres** RESTAURANT & XIAO CHI BAR

Sustainable, Modern, Chinese Cuisine

Pearl District, Portland
Since 2002

Bring in your in-bound Alaska Airlines boarding pass for a complimentary cocktail or appetizer.

971-222-7327
seresrestaurant.com
1105 NW Lovejoy St, Portland, OR

Seres Restaurant and Bar sources the freshest local and organic ingredients for its beautifully presented Sichuan-style Chinese Cuisine.

Seres

Seres Restaurant, formally Sungari Pearl, is located in the Pearl District and has been serving the greater Portland area since 2002. Seres Restaurant features modern Chinese cuisine with emphasis on fresh, local ingredients.

Seres' dishes feature ingredients such as local organic produce, Oregon's Painted Hills Natural Beef, fresh Oregon-caught razor clams and Dungeness crab, and bean curd from Portland's own OTA Tofu Company. Chefs at Seres prepare dishes with lower sodium and no added MSG. They believe Chinese cuisine can be delicious and good for you, and take pride in preparing locally sourced, delicious, made-to-order Chinese, specializing in preparing dishes to meet different types of dietary restrictions. For example, Seres offers diners an entire gluten-free menu as well as gluten-free items during happy hour – with gluten-free soy sauce on request.

You will still find every traditional long-loved Chinese food like fried rice, potstickers, or Kung Pao chicken at Seres, however with a lightness and purity that are not only delicious, but important.

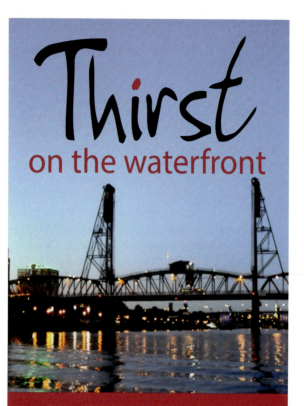

Thirst Bistro

Highlighting Pacific NW ingredients paired with local wines, craft brews and spirits.

Enjoy gorgeous views of the Willamette River, Bridges and Mt Hood from the Bistro or outside patio. Full dining menu features local ingredients supporting local purveyors. The Happy Hour menu is vast and has daily specials. Thirsty Tuesday is $48 for two people – and includes an appetizer, entrée, dessert and bottle of wine!

The Wine Spectator award-winning Pacific-NW-focused wine list specializes in the Willamette Valley, Walla Walla, Rogue Valley, Columbia Gorge and other Pacific NW AVAs. Whether it is a winery with a cult following like Domaine Drouhan, Sineann, Willakenzie, Sokol-Blosser, Owen Roe or Beaux Frères – or a smaller, up and coming winery like Dumas Station, Et Fille, Biggio Hamina and more – they scour the Pacific NW for the best wines. List rotates frequently so you can always try something new – try a wine flight!

Three private party spaces with no space fee. All have floor-to-ceiling windows and the entire space can be bought out for parties up to 150. The attached bottle/gift shop highlights products from the Pacific NW. Take wine or beer to go by the bottle or growler.

For more information including private events:
www.thirstbistro.com   (503) 295-2747

10 Years of Perfect 10s!

I myself, was surprised to find that since 2007, there have been only FIVE places that have rated a "Perfect 10" in all 10 editions of my book!

Many have tried, and many have failed, so please join me in saying BIG KUDOS to these forerunners! Give this crew a big high five, and go visit again...

Bartini (2108 NW Glisan)
Giant menu of 25 items and 50% off all martinis!
See review on page 126.

La Calaca Comelona (2304 SE Belmont)
Such great Mexican food, lots of it, and *deals!*
See review on page 173.

Oba (555 NW 12th Ave.)
My second-ever Happy Hour. I remain in love!
See review on page 196.

Salty's (3839 NE Marine Dr.)
The view! And with such good food to match!
See review on page 219.

Uptown Billiards Club (120 NW 23rd Ave)
The least talked-about, but most talented chef!
See review on page 243.

Kings of Happy Hour

You know 'em, you love 'em. But I didn't feel like I'd be telling you anything you didn't already know even if I did full reviews. If you haven't made it to these basic stellar starters yet, go!

RESTAURANTS UNLIMITED

Henry's Tavern
3:00–6:00pm/10:00pm–close Daily; ★All day Sun

Newport Seafood Grill
3:00-6:00pm Daily (on a pier/closes for the winter)

Prime Rib & Chocolate Cake
4:00pm-close Daily. Bar menu and daly specials.

Stanford's
3:00–6:00pm/9:00pm–close Daily; ★All day Sun

Manzana / Portland City Grill (See p.180 & 209)

LANDRY'S, INC.

Charthouse 4:00–7:00pm Daily

Claim Jumper 4:00-5:30pm Daily

Heathman 4:00–6:00pm Daily

Morton's 4:30pm-6:30pm Daily; 4:30pm-close Sun

McCormick's & Schmick's (See p.37 & 183)
Jake's Famous / Jake's Grill (See p.169 & 170)

Everyone's Favorite Neighbors

North 45
Year-Round Patio.
Global menu sourcing local ingredients.
Perfect for date night or game night.
Lunch & dinner. Daily happy hour, Monday All Night.
517 NW 21st
www.north45pub.com p.193

Paddy's Bar & Grill
Portland's Oldest Irish Pub! More than 600 spirits.
Traditional Irish fare with Northwest ingredients.
Lunch, dinner, daily happy hour.
65 SW Yamhill
www.paddys.com p.199

Circa 33
Prohibition Style Cocktails. 100+ whiskeys.
Daily happy hour, Monday All Night.
(Ask what's behind the bookcase!)
3348 SE Belmont
www.circa33.com p.142

The Station
Seven screens to watch the game. Dog friendly patio.
Daily happy hour, Tuesday All Night.
2703 NE Alberta
www.thestationpdx.com p.228

Produce Row Café
Pouring 24 taps. Year-Round Patio.
Portland's Original Curated Craft Beer House since 1974.
Lunch & dinner. Daily happy hour, Monday All Night.
204 SE Oak
www.producerowcafe.com p.213

Ask about catering at our places or yours.
www.eatanddrinkpdx.com

IRC Independent Restaurant Concepts

"Golden Tickets"

COUPONS

*Presented in mostly alphabetical order :-)

Coupons *are provided as a courtesy. Menus may change or restaurants may close, and neither the author nor the publisher makes any warranty or representation about the validity or enforceability of the coupons. Originals only. May not be good on holidays. Please use coupons wisely — and nicely. Remember to tip on full total before discounts. And always consider number of trips to the table when calculating. That extra dollar or two goes a long way to brighten your server's day!*

23 Hoyt
529 NW 23rd Ave.
Portland, OR 97210
(503) 445-7400
www.23hoyt.com

Buy any two dinner entrees and get $10.00 taken off your total bill. Cannot be combined with any other offer, Happy Hour, or specials. Limit $10.00 off per coupon, one coupon per table. Expires 12/30/16.

Altabira
1021 NE Grand Ave. #600
Portland, OR 97232
(503) 963-3600
www.altabira.com

Enjoy a delicious Citizen Baker pretzel -- free! Redeemable at Altabira Restaurant only. Requires food purchase of equal or greater value. Good at any time including Happy Hour. Limit one free pretzel per coupon. Limit two coupons per table. Expires 12/30/16.

Amalfi's Restaurant & Mercato
4703 NE Fremont
Portland, OR 97213
(503) 284-6747
www.amalfisrestaurant.com

Buy any Happy Hour food menu item and get receive a complimentary Happy Hour pizza! Valid only during Happy Hour. Not good with any other offer or take-out. Limit one free happy hour menu item per coupon. Limit two coupons per table. Beverage purchase required. Expires 12/30/16.

Amalfi's Restaurant & Mercato
4703 NE Fremont
Portland, OR 97213
(503) 284-6747
www.amalfisrestaurant.com

An Italian-inspired marketplace specializing in fresh house-made foods, local delicacies and Italian-imported products. grab-n-go pastas, salads, pizzas, wine... Dinner is done!

*Free Mercato salad with purchase of a Mercato take & bake pizza. Not good with any other offer or discount.
One coupon per visit. Expires 12/30/16.*

Bluehour Restaurant

250 NW 13th Avenue
Portland OR 97209
503-226-3394
www.bluehouronline.com

Buy any two dinner entrees and get $10.00 taken off your total bill. Cannot be combined with any other offer, Happy Hour, or specials. Limit $10.00 off per coupon, one coupon per table. Expires 12/30/16.

Bazi Bierbrasserie

1522 SE 32nd Ave.
Portland, OR 97214
(503) 234-8888
www.bazipdx.com

Buy any Happy Hour food menu item and get one of equal or lesser value free! Valid only during Happy Hour. Not good with any other offer or take-out. Limit one free happy hour menu item per coupon. Limit two coupons per table. Beverage purchase required. Expires 12/30/16.

2016 Superstar Cover fave!

Bellino
1230 NW Hoyt
Portland, OR 97209
(503) 208-2992
www.bellinoportland.com

Buy any two dinner entrees and get $10.00 taken off your total bill. Cannot be combined with any other offer, Happy Hour, or specials. Limit $10.00 off per coupon, one coupon per table. Expires 12/30/16.

Recommended

The Benson Hotel's Palm Court
309 SW Broadway
Portland, OR 97205
(503) 228-2000
www.bensonhotel.com

Get 30% off your total food bill at lunch or dinner in the Palm Court Restaurant or Lounge. Cannot be combined with any other offer, Happy Hour, or specials. Limit one coupon per table. Expires 12/30/16.

Clarklewis
1001 SE Water Ave.
Portland, OR 97214
(503) 235-2294
www.clarklewispdx.com

Buy any two dinner entrees and get $10.00 taken off your total bill. Cannot be combined with any other offer, Happy Hour, or specials. Limit $10.00 off per coupon, one coupon per table. Expires 12/30/16.

Chez Machin
3553 SE Hawthorne Blvd.
Portland, OR 97214
(503) 736-9381
www.chezmachin.com

Enjoy a cup of French onion soup -- free! Requires food purchase of equal or greater value. Good at any time including Happy Hour. Limit one free soup per coupon. Limit two coupons per table. Expires 12/30/16.

Cellar 55 Tasting Room
1812 Washington St.
Vancouver, WA 98660
(360) 693-2700
www.cellar55tastingroom.com

While you are sipping a glass of one of our craft wines, why not nibble on a charcuterie or cheese platter, too? Get half-off a platter from our tasting room. Maximum $20.00 platter before discount. Beverage purchase required. Expires 12/30/16.

Circa 33
3348 SE Belmont
Portland, OR 97214
(503) 477-7682
www.circa33.com

Enjoy a free appetizer ($10.00 or less) when you purchase any two dinner entrees or sandwiches. Cannot be combined with any other offer, Happy Hour, or specials. Limit $10.00 off per coupon, one coupon per table. Expires 12/30/16.

DarSalam
2921 NE Alberta St.
Portland, OR 97211
503-206-6148
www.darsalamportland.com

Enjoy a serving of our signature beet salad -- free! Requires food purchase of equal or greater value. Good at any time including Happy Hour. Limit one free salad per coupon. Limit two coupons per table. Expires 12/30/16.

DarSalam Lazurdi
320 SW Alder St.
Portland, OR 97204
503-444-7813
www.darsalamportland.com

Enjoy a serving of our signature beet salad -- free! Requires food purchase of equal or greater value. Good at any time including Happy Hour. Limit one free salad per coupon. Limit two coupons per table. Expires 12/30/16.

Equinox Restaurant

830 N Shaver St
Portland, OR 97227
(503) 460-3333
www.equinoxrestaurantpdx.com

Buy one select brunch entree and get one of equal or lesser value free! Maximum value $10.00. Wed-Sun 9:00am-2:00pm (schedule subject to change). Not good with any other offer or take-out. One free brunch menu item per coupon. Limit one coupon per table. Expires 12/30/16.

Equinox Restaurant

830 N Shaver St
Portland, OR 97227
(503) 460-3333
www.equinoxrestaurantpdx.com

Buy any Happy Hour food menu item and get one of equal or lesser value free! Valid only during Happy Hour. Not good with any other offer or take-out. Limit one free Happy Hour menu item per coupon. Limit two coupons per table. Beverage purchase required. Expires 12/30/16.

Grant House

1101 Officers Row
Vancouver, WA 98661
(360) 906-1101
www.thegranthouse.us

Buy any Happy Hour food menu item and get one of equal or lesser value free! Valid only during Happy Hour. Not good with any other offer or take-out. Limit one free Happy Hour menu item per coupon. Limit two coupons per table. Beverage purchase required. Expires 12/30/16.

Iconic

2226 NE Broadway
Portland, OR 97232
(503) 946-1621
www.iconiclounge.com

Get a free order of our award-winning mac & cheese with purchase of another food item of equal or greater value! Valid any time. Not good with any other offer or take-out. Limit two coupons per table, one free order per coupon. Beverage purchase required. Expires 12/30/16.

Jantzen Beach Bar & Grill

909 N Hayden Island Drive
Portland, OR 97217
(503) 978-4554
www.redlion.com/jantzen-beach/dining

Buy one dinner entree and get one of equal or lesser value free! Not good with any other offer or take-out.
One free dinner entree per coupon.
Limit one coupon per table. Expires 12/30/16.

Karam Lebanese & Syrian Cuisine

515 SW 4th Ave.
Portland, OR 97204
(503) 223-0830
www.karamsrestaurant.com

Enjoy one of our mezza plates at half-price! Valid any time. Not good with any other offer or take-out. Limit one coupon per table, one half-priced plate per coupon.
Beverage purchase required. Expires 12/30/16.

La Calaca Comelona

2304 SE Belmont
Portland, OR 97214
(503) 239-9675
www.lacalacacomelona.com

Buy any food menu item and get a free mini-quesadilla. We know you'll fall in love with them! Valid any time. Not good with any other offer or take-out. Expires 12/30/16.

Las Primas

3971 N Williams Ave #103
Portland, OR 97227
(503) 206-5790
lasprimaskitchen.com

Buy any Happy Hour food menu item and get one of equal or lesser value free! Valid only during Happy Hour. Not good with any other offer or take-out. Limit one free Happy Hour menu item per coupon. Limit two coupons per table. Beverage purchase required. Expires 12/30/16.

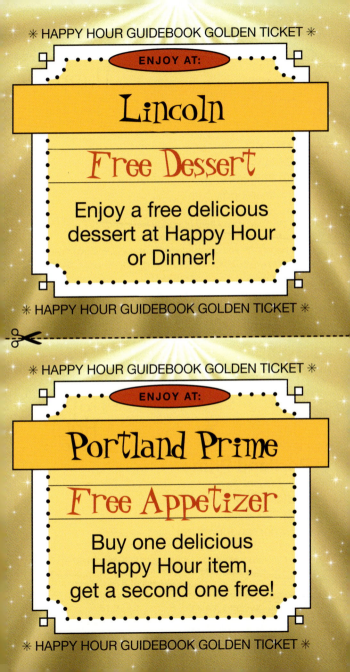

Happy Hour
-- GUIDEBOOK --
Recommended

Lincoln
3808 N Williams Ave.
(503) 288-6200
www.lincolnpdx.com

Buy any food menu item at Happy Hour or dinner and get a free dessert! Does not include cheese plate. Not good with any other offer or take-out. Limit one free dessert per coupon, one coupon per table. Expires 12/30/16.

Happy Hour
-- GUIDEBOOK --
2016 Superstar Cover fave!

Portland Prime
121 SW 3rd Ave.
Portland, OR 97204
(503) 223-6200
www.portlandprime.net

Buy any Happy Hour food menu item and get one of equal or lesser value free! Valid only during Happy Hour. Not good with any other offer or take-out. Limit one free Happy Hour menu item per coupon. Limit two coupons per table. Beverage purchase required. Expires 12/30/16.

Mama Mia Trattoria
439 SW 2nd Avenue
Portland, OR 97204
(503) 295-6464
www.mamamiatrattoria.com

Buy one brunch entree and get one of equal or lesser value free. Maximum value $12.00. Not good with any other offer or take-out. One free brunch menu item per coupon. One coupon per table. Expires 12/30/16.

Mama Mia Trattoria
439 SW 2nd Avenue
Portland, OR 97204
(503) 295-6464
www.mamamiatrattoria.com

Buy any two dinner entrees and get $10.00 taken off your total bill. Cannot be combined with any other offer, Happy Hour, or specials. Limit $10.00 off per coupon, one coupon per table. Expires 12/30/16.

Manzana
305 1st Street
Lake Oswego, OR 97034
(503) 675-3322
www.manzanagrill.com

Buy any Happy Hour food menu item and get one of equal or lesser value free! Valid only during Happy Hour. Not good with any other offer or take-out. Limit one free Happy Hour menu item per coupon. Limit two coupons per table. Beverage purchase required. Expires 12/30/16.

Mother's
212 SW Stark St.
Portland, OR 97204
(503) 464-1122
www.mothersbistro.com

Buy any Happy Hour food menu item and get one of equal or lesser value free! Valid only during Happy Hour. Not good with any other offer or take-out. Limit one free Happy Hour menu item per coupon. Limit two coupons per table. Beverage purchase required. Expires 12/30/16.

Happy Hour
-- GUIDEBOOK --
Recommended

Night Light
2100 SE Clinton
Portland, OR 97202
(503) 731-6500
www.nightlightlounge.net

Buy any Happy Hour food menu item and get one of equal or lesser value free! Valid only during Happy Hour. Not good with any other offer or take-out. Limit one free Happy Hour menu item per coupon. Limit two coupons per table. Beverage purchase required. Expires 12/30/16.

Happy Hour
-- GUIDEBOOK --
Recommended

North Light
3746 N Mississippi Ave.
Portland, OR 97227
(503) 477-7079
www.northlightpdx.com

Good for the whole table – bring your friends! Offer is for food only and does not include drink deals outside of our standard Happy Hour time. Not good with any other offer or take-out. Beverage purchase required. Expires 12/30/16.

2016 Superstar Cover fave!

North 45
517 NW 21st Ave.
Portland, OR 97209
(503) 248-6317
www.north45pub.com

Enjoy a free appetizer ($10.00 or less) when you purchase any two dinner entrees or sandwiches. Cannot be combined with any other offer, Happy Hour, or specials. Limit $10.00 off per coupon, one coupon per table. Expires 12/30/16.

Happy Hour
-- GUIDEBOOK --
Recommended

Paddy's
65 SW Yamhill St.
Portland, OR 97204
503-224-5626
www.paddys.com

Buy one lunch entree or sandwich and get one of equal or lesser value FREE! Cannot be combined with any other offer, Happy Hour, or specials. Limit one free entree per coupon, one coupon per table. Not valid on St. Patrick's Day. Expires 12/30/16.

Piattino
1140 NW Everett
Portland, OR 97209
(971) 983-8000
www.piattinopdx.com

Take 25% off any pizza, any time! Not good with any other offer or take-out. Limit one pizza special per coupon. Two coupons per table. Beverage purchase required. Expires 12/30/16.

Pine Shed Ribs
17730 Pilkington Rd.
Lake Oswego, OR 97035
(503) 635-7427
www.pineshedribs.com

Buy any food menu item and get a free slider plate! Valid only at Happy Hour (adding bacon is suggested but is $2.00 extra). Not good with any other offer or take-out. Limit three free sliders per coupon. Limit one coupon per table. Beverage purchase required. Expires 12/30/16.

Pink Rose

1300 NW Lovejoy
Portland, OR 97209
(503) 482-2165
www.pinkrosepdx.com

Buy any Happy Hour food menu item and get one of equal or lesser value free! Valid only during Happy Hour. Not good with any other offer or take-out. Limit one free Happy Hour menu item per coupon. Limit two coupons per table. Beverage purchase required. Expires 12/30/16.

Pour Wine Bar

2755 NE Broadway
Portland, OR 97232
(503) 288-7687
www.pourwinebar.com

Get a free cheese plate when you purchase any bottle of wine! Not good with any other offer or take-out. Limit one free cheese plate per coupon. Limit one coupon per table. Expires 12/30/16.

Produce Row Cafe
204 SE Oak St.
Portland, OR 97214
(503) 232-8355
www.producerowcafe.com

Enjoy a free appetizer ($10.00 or less) when you purchase any two lunch or dinner entrees or sandwiches. Cannot be combined with any other offer, Happy Hour, or specials. Limit $10.00 off per coupon, one coupon per table. Expires 12/30/16.

The Station
2703 NE Alberta
Portland, OR 97211
(503) 284-4491
www.stationpdx.com

Enjoy a free appetizer ($10.00 or less) when you purchase any two dinner entrees or sandwiches. Cannot be combined with any other offer, Happy Hour, or specials. Limit $10.00 off per coupon, one coupon per table. Expires 12/30/16.

Salty's on the Columbia
3839 NE Marine Drive
Portland, OR
(503) 288-4444
www.saltys.com/portland

Buy any two entrees at lunch or dinner and get $10.00 taken off your total bill. Cannot be combined with any other offer, Happy Hour, or specials. Limit $10.00 off per coupon, one coupon per table. Expires 12/30/16.

Saucebox
214 SW Broadway
Portland, OR 97209
(503) 241-3393
www.saucebox.com

Buy any two dinner entrees and get $10.00 taken off your total bill. Cannot be combined with any other offer, Happy Hour, or specials. Limit $10.00 off per coupon, one coupon per table. Expires 12/30/16.

Seres Restaurant
1105 NW Lovejoy
Portland, OR 97209
(971) 222-0100
www.seresrestaurant.com

Buy one lunch or dinner entree and get one of equal or lesser value free. Not good with any other offer or take-out. One free entree per coupon. One coupon per table. Expires 12/30/16.

Seres Restaurant
1105 NW Lovejoy
Portland, OR 97209
(971) 222-0100
www.seresrestaurant.com

Buy any Small Plate menu item and get one of equal or lesser value free! Valid lunch, Happy Hour, or dinner. Not good with any other offer or take-out. Limit one free menu item per coupon. Limit two coupons per table. Beverage purchase required. Expires 12/30/16.

Slide Inn
2348 SE Ankeny
Portland, OR 97214
(503) 236-4997
www.slideinnpdx.com

Buy any Happy Hour food menu item and get one of equal or lesser value free! Valid only during Happy Hour. Not good with any other offer or take-out. Limit one free Happy Hour menu item per coupon. Limit two coupons per table. Beverage purchase required. Expires 12/30/16.

Streetcar Bistro
1101 NW Northrup
Portland, OR 97209
(503) 227-2988
www.streetcarbistro.com

Get a free order of our famously fabulous bacon-wrapped dates with purchase of another food item (of equal or greater value)! Valid any time. Not good with any other offer or take-out. Limit two coupons per table, one free order per coupon. Beverage purchase required. Expires 12/30/16.

Salvador Molly's
1523 SW Sunset Blvd.
Portland, OR 97239
(503) 293-1790
www.salvadormollys.com

Buy any Happy Hour food menu item and get one of equal or lesser value free! Valid only during Happy Hour. Not good with any other offer or take-out. Limit one free Happy Hour menu item per coupon. Limit two coupons per table. Beverage purchase required. Expires 12/30/16.

Tapalaya
28 NE 28th Ave.
Portland, OR 97232
(503) 232-6652
www.tapalaya.com

Buy any appetizer or entree at lunch, happy hour, or dinner, and enjoy a free bowl of our delicious housemade spicy bayou chips. Not good with any other offer or take out. One free bowl of chips per coupon. Limit two free bowls per table. Expires 12/30/16.

Thai Bloom NW
333 NW 23rd Ave
Portland, OR 97210
(503) 243-7557
www.thaibloomrestaurant.com

Buy one lunch or dinner entree and get a free scoop of our delicious housemade coconut ice cream. Not good with any other offer or take-out. One free scoop per coupon. Limit two coupons per table. Expires 12/30/16.

Thai Bloom Beaverton
3800 SW Cedar Hills Blvd
Beaverton, OR 97005
(503) 644-8010
www.thaibloomrestaurant.com

Buy one lunch or dinner entree and get a free scoop of our delicious housemade coconut ice cream. Not good with any other offer or take-out. One free scoop per coupon. Limit two coupons per table. Expires 12/30/16.

Thirst Wine Bar & Bistro
0315 SW Montgomery St
Portland, OR 97201
(503) 295-2747
www.thirstwinebar.com

Buy any Happy Hour food menu item and get one of equal or lesser value free! Valid only during Happy Hour. Not good with any other offer or take-out. Limit one free Happy Hour menu item per coupon. Limit two coupons per table. Beverage purchase required. Expires 12/30/16.

Thirst Wine Bar & Bistro
0315 SW Montgomery St
Portland, OR 97201
(503) 295-2747
www.thirstwinebar.com

Buy any Happy Hour food menu item and get one of equal or lesser value free! Valid only during Happy Hour. Not good with any other offer or take-out. Limit one free Happy Hour menu item per coupon. Limit two coupons per table. Beverage purchase required. Expires 12/30/16.

Tavern on Kruse
4835 Meadows Rd #133
Lake Oswego, OR 97035
(503) 303-5280
www.tavernonkruse.com

Buy any Happy Hour food menu item and get one of equal or lesser value free! Valid only during Happy Hour. Not good with any other offer or take-out. Limit one free Happy Hour menu item per coupon. Limit two coupons per table. Beverage purchase required. Expires 12/30/16.

Trader Vic's
1203 NW Glisan
Portland, OR 97209
(503) 467-2277
www.tradervicspdx.com

Buy any Happy Hour food menu item and get one of equal or lesser value free! Valid only during Happy Hour. Not good with any other offer or take-out. Limit one free Happy Hour menu item per coupon. Limit two coupons per table. Beverage purchase required. Expires 12/30/16.

Happy Hour
-- GUIDEBOOK --
Recommended

Uptown Billiards
120 NW 23rd Ave.
Portland, OR 97210
(503) 226-6909
www.uptownbilliards.com

Coupon good for one hour of free pool on one table.
Minimum $10 food purchase required.
Not redeemable for cash. Expires 12/30/16.

Happy Hour
-- GUIDEBOOK --
Recommended

Via Delizia
1105 NW Marshall
Portland, OR 97209
(503) 225-9300
www.viadelizia.com

Buy any two dinner entrees and get $10.00 taken off your total bill. Cannot be combined with any other offer, Happy Hour, or specials. Limit $10.00 off per coupon, one coupon per table. Expires 12/30/16.

Wild Abandon

2411 SE Belmont
Portland, OR 97214
(503) 232-4458
wildabandonrestaurant.com

Buy any Happy Hour food menu item and get one of equal or lesser value free! Valid only during Happy Hour. Not good with any other offer or take-out. Limit one free Happy Hour menu item per coupon. Limit two coupons per table. Beverage purchase required. Expires 12/30/16.

XV

15 SW 2nd Ave.
Portland, OR 97204
(503) 790-9090
www.barfifteen.com

Buy any Happy Hour food menu item and get one of equal or lesser value free! Valid only during Happy Hour. Not good with any other offer or take-out. Limit one free Happy Hour menu item per coupon. Limit two coupons per table. Beverage purchase required. Expires 12/30/16.

Live happy!
Share. Care. Be kind. Give. Love.

The Happy Mermaid
GIFT SHOP/GALLERY

Hayden Island / 250 NE Tomahawk Island Dr.
Open Daily April 9–Oct 8 | Noon-Sunset

www.thehappymermaid.com

The Happy Mermaid
250 NE Tomahawk Island Drive
On the Columbia River / Hayden Island
Portland, Oregon 97217
(971) 285-7100
www.thehappymermaid.com

Portland's cutest gift shop – and it floats! Owned by me, Cindy Anderson, the author of the Happy Hour Guidebook :-)

Open seasonally April 9-Oct. 8, 2016 (when it's nice outside). Spend at least $40 (not including $15 book price) and get a FREE Happy Hour Guidebook! They make the best gifts! Not good with any other offer or discount. Limit one free book/one coupon per visit. Expires 10/8/16.

The Happy Mermaid
250 NE Tomahawk Island Drive
On the Columbia River / Hayden Island
Portland, Oregon 97217
(971) 285-7100
www.thehappymermaid.com

Portland's cutest gift shop – and it floats! Owned by me, Cindy Anderson, the author of the Happy Hour Guidebook :-)

Open seasonally April 9-Oct. 8, 2016 (when it's nice outside). Buy at least $25 worth of merchandise, get $5.00 off your purchase! Not good with any other offer or discount. One coupon per visit. Expires 10/8/16.

The Arrangement
4210 NE Fremont
Portland, OR 97213
(503) 287-4440
www.thearrangementpdx.com

*Locally owned. Local artists. Locally loved. Est. 1980.
Gift wrapping and card selection are a specialty!*

Valid for in-store purchase only. Not good with any other offer or discount. Offer good on purchase of one individual item. One coupon per visit. Expires 12/30/16.

Gumbo Gifts & Gallery
3900 N Mississippi Ave.
Portland, OR 97227
(971) 703-4345
www.gumbogiftsandgallery.com

"Feed your imagination with curious delights!" Gifts, jewelry, hats, scarves, novelty glasses, toys, socks, music and so much more!

Buy at least $25 worth of merchandise, get $5.00 off your purchase! Not good with any other offer or discount. One coupon per visit. Expires 12/30/16.

Oblation Papers & Press
516 NW 12th Ave.
Portland, Oregon 97209
(503) 223-1093
www.oblationpapers.com

European-style paper boutique and letterpress studio, offering fine papers, artful cards and ephemera.

Buy at least $25 worth of merchandise, get $5.00 off your purchase! Not good with any other offer or discount. One coupon per visit. Valid for in-store gift purchases only (offer not available for online purchases). Expires 12/30/16.

Stella's
1108 NW 21st Ave.
Portland, OR 97209
(503) 295-5930
www.stellason21st.com

Like the city we live in, we're classy, but unpretentious. And like Portland, you'll find many unexpected surprises. Careful attention to detail. First-rate quality.

Buy at least $25 worth of merchandise, get $5.00 off your purchase! Not good with any other offer or discount. One coupon per visit. Expires 12/30/16.

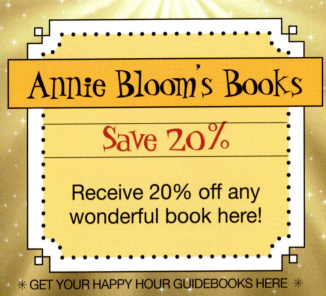

Annie Bloom's Books
7834 SW Capitol Hwy
Portland, OR 97219
(503) 246-0053
www.annieblooms.com

Valid for in-store purchase only. Not good with any other offer or discount. Offer good on purchase of one book. One coupon per visit. Expires 12/30/16.

Broadway Books
1714 NE Broadway
Portland, OR 97232
503-284-1726
www.broadwaybooks.net

Valid for in-store purchase only. Not good with any other offer or discount. Offer good on purchase of one book. One coupon per visit. Expires 12/30/16.

Reviews

★ Rating System ★

As fun as this so-called *job* is, I take it very seriously. I am in a unique positon of having personally analyzed literally hundreds of Happy Hours, and have devised a formula to rate Happy Hours in comparison to others. You'll see little bold numbers in each category, and this is how I judge:

Food

Exclusively focused on food served at Happy Hour only. Considers taste, discounts, healthy alternatives and uniqueness (i.e. not the usual bar menu).

3 – Delicious food, lots of options and dood discounts
2 – Pretty good food and/or discount.
1 – Negligible discounts, few selections, or possibly bad taste. It will be explained in that section.

Drinks

It's not all about being the cheapest, but need deals! Quality and number of options are also factored in.

3 – Good deals, variety, and quality drinks.
2 – Pretty good, but need more variety or discounts.
1 – Eh. Not that impressed. Not trying or expensive.

Atmosphere

Looks matter! As a rule, this book covers the nicer places in town. Good vibes? Stunning decor? What?

3 – Upscale and unique decor and/or gorgeous views.
2 – Nice enough, but not quite stunning.
1 – More of a bar than a restaurant. Low on style and decor. Women may be uncomfortable when alone.

SAT-SUN

23 Hoyt

NW/Nob Hill Map
529 NW 23rd Ave.
(503) 445-7400
www.23hoyt.com

Happy Hours
4:00–6:30pm Daily; 9:00pm–Midnight Fri–Sat

Food Deals 3
$2.00–$9.00
Nearly 20 menu items that will vary seasonally: cheeseburgers, salads, mac & cheese, flatbreads, mushrooms, squash tempura, corndogs, and dare I say the best deviled eggs in the city!

Drink Specials 3
$5.00 drafts; $5.00 select wines
$5.00-$7.00 specialty cocktails

Atmosphere 3
Sleek, stylish and soaring inside with lofted areas overlooking the bar. Cool and contemporary design, yet remains warm and inviting. Floor-to-ceiling windows, slate grays, natural wood tables, fresh flowers – and trees. Stellar!

Why I Really Like It
It's a solidly impressive Happy Hour, as all of owner Bruce Carey's places are (Bluehour, Clarklewis, Saucebox). Simple but perfect, every time.

SAT-SUN

Altabira

New!

~ 2016 ~
TOP 10
Superstar

Central East Side
1021 NE Grand Avenue #600
(503) 963-3600
www.altabira.com

Happy Hours
4:00-6:00pm Daily

GOLDEN TICKET!

Food Deals 3
$4.00-$7.00
Alternatives perfect to pair with beer or wine: Three kinds of pizza, cheeseburger, brisket sandwich, field greens salad, fries, mussels, wings, soup, or a big Citizen Baker pretzel.

Drink Specials 3
$4.00 local drafts; $5.00 wines
$5.00 well drinks; $6.00 cocktail special

Atmosphere 3+
Wow! What a stunning space! Formerly the old and dark Windows at the Red Lion, but you'd never know it. Light and bright, and ultra-modern, with a big central bar, large windows all around, and a killer patio! An immediate fave.

New this Year/First Impressions
I'm in love with the giant patio, views, firepits and excellent contemporary design throughout!
I also love the rotating, well-selected craft beer list. It's kind of city-cool, and my kind of perfect!

SAT-SUN

Amalfi's

~ 2016 ~
TOP 10
Superstar

Fremont Map
4703 NE Fremont St.
(503) 284-6747
www.amalfisrestaurant.com

Happy Hours
4:00–6:00pm and 9:00pm-close Tues-Sun
(from 3:00pm Sat-Sun)

GOLDEN TICKET!

Food Deals 3
$4.00-$6.00
Enjoy over a dozen zesty Italian eats: three kinds of mini pizzas, lotsa pastas/raviolis, meatballs, shrimp scampi, soup, salad, bruschetta, prawns.

Drink Specials
No discounts, but always have $4.00-$5.00 beer; $5.00 house wines; $7.00-$8.00 cocktails (and a hysterical and creatively-named cocktail list!)

Atmosphere 3
For more than 50 years, Amalfi's has served up some of Portland's best Italian food, and is still to this day, a much-beloved icon. Comfy yet contemporary, romantic and still social. Table-top fireplaces both inside and out. Great patio! They also have a super-cute, in-house Italian Mercato.

Why I Really Like It
Happy Hour of the Year 2011! It fits the bill for so many occasions, whether it's a night out with friends, first date, or 50th Anniversary.

SAT-SUN/ALL MON

Aquariva

Willamette River
0470 SW Hamilton Ct.
(503) 802-5850
www.riversedgehotel.com

Happy Hours
3:00–6:30pm Daily; ★All night Monday

Food Deals 3
$3.00–$6.00
A switch up in menu to the more traditional side of bar food with items like loaded fries, nuts, pork tacos, mac & cheese, wings, lamb chili, salads.

Drink Specials 3
$4.50 select beer; $5.00 red or white wine
$6.00 cocktail of the day
$4.00 Portland's favorite "Build your own" Bloody Mary bar at Sunday brunch

Atmosphere 3
Totally striking architecture and design delight and captivate upon entrance, and draw you in to find that resplendent river views await! Ultra-contemporary with comfy couch pits, cocktail tables and soaring ceilings. Outside patio too.

Why I Really Like It
Fancy and beautiful but without the high prices to match. And I love the river view too! Enjoy a water's edge walk before or after.

Aviary

Alberta Map
1733 NE Alberta
(503) 287-2400
www.aviarypdx.com

Happy Hours
5:00–7:00pm Mon-Fri

Food Deals 3
$2.00-$6.00
You are in for a treat! Happy Hour is taken up a notch with a very unique and eclectic, seasonal menu with items like tempura green beans, Brussels sprouts nachos, slaw dog, pulled pork sliders, deviled eggs, trotter n eggs, and oysters. Check out the dinner menu before biting on HH!

Drink Specials 3
$3.00 drafts; $5.00 house wines
$5.00 wells; $6.00 daily cocktail specials

Atmosphere 3
Happy Hour is inside all the way in the back in the very cool, dark, and cozy bar area, or out front on the plaza-style, street-side patio. One of Portland's top "chef-driven" restaurants!

Why I Really Like It
A foodie sanctuary. Cozy and cool! Or hot and fun, depending on where you sit and our always interesting Portland weather. It's a classic.

SAT-SUN

Bacchus Bar

Downtown (East)
422 SW Broadway
(503) 228-1212
www.hotelvintage-portland.com

Happy Hours
4:00-6:00pm Daily

Food Deals 3
$3.00-$9.00
Half-off all food! Save big on small plates like salads, fondue, chicken croquettes, clams or beef tartare; plus half-off burgers, pasta or pizza.

Drink Specials 0
Sadly, no drink deals

Atmosphere 3
Cool space! It's part of the lobby of the renovated Hotel Vintage that also houses Pazzo (which no longer hosts Happy Hour). Totally swanky and mod with a blackboard rendering of wine info, high-tech wall of wine, a glowing bar, and open white columns shooting up to the 2nd floor where you'll find pool tables and another lounge.

New this Year/First Impressions
A totally different, ultra-contemporary look, especially in comparison to the traditional style of Pazzo. It's several bars in one and a fun place to drink wine or enjoy a craft cocktail.

Bamboo Sushi

NW/Nob Hill / Alberta / Southeast
836 NW 23rd Ave; (971) 229-1925
1409 NE Alberta St.
310 SE 28th Ave; (503) 232-5255
www.bamboosushipdx.com

Happy Hours
5:00-6:00pm Mon–Fri (from 4:30 other locations)

Food Deals 3
$3.00–$7.00
The food at Bamboo Sushi is soooo goood! To list in plain English: house-pickled veggies, seafood pancake, seaweed salad, mushrooms, salad, veggie-tofu-crisped noodles, grilled peppers, plus nigiri set, daily hand rolls, and veggie rolls.

Drink Specials 3
$3.00 Sapporo; $5.00 wine; $4.00–$7.00 sake

Atmosphere 3
The three different locations are quite similar in layout and overall style. Serene and cozy with focus on sustainability and Japanese simplicity. Natural, neutral woods, pillows on bench seating and fascinating artwork. Happy Hour is in the lounge areas only.

Why I Really Like It
The food! And the drinks. But really, the food!!!

Bartini

SAT-SUN

A PERFECT 10
TEN YEARS
– and counting –

NW/Nob Hill Map
2108 NW Glisan
(503) 224-7919
www.bartinipdx.com

Happy Hours
4:00–6:30pm and 9:30pm–close Daily
4:00pm–close Sunday and Monday★
9:30pm–close Fri-Sat (food only)

Food Deals 3+
$3.00–$4.00
Literally 25 gourmet choices, plus fondue! They have several salad types, sliders (choice of three kinds), crab cakes, coconut shrimp, shrimp tacos, a number of flatbreads, a variety of satays, burgers, hummus, tacos, mashed potato martini.

Drink Specials 3+
Half off signature martinis (full menu of about 100 different kinds – really!)

Atmosphere 3
Black, black and more black; small & intimate martini lounge; best appreciated after sunset. Truly a classic and all-time fave of so many fans! Sidewalk seating at Happy Hour.

Why I Really Like It
It's a crazy-good Happy Hour! One of only five places with a Perfect 10 score since 2007. Love!

Barlow

Downtown (East) Map
737 SW Salmon
(503) 227-0705
www.barlowpdx.com

Happy Hours
3:00-6:00pm and 10:00pm-close Mon-Sat

Food Deals 2
$4.00-$8.00
Tiny retro sipping nibbles like popcorn, pimento cheese dip, tomato soup with grilled cheese, charcuterie & cheese plate, and Brussels sprouts.

Drink Specials 2
$5.00 drafts; $7.00 wine; $6.00 wells
$8.00 cocktail of the day

Atmosphere 3+
From the owners of the Picnic House next door, a strikingly beautiful cocktail lounge that bows to the heydays of theater and the nearby Broadway district. Sit at the bar for impressive shows of cocktail artistry – and better service if crowded. Their name in lights, Barlow means flapper in 1920s slang. Such a gorgeous place!

Why I Really Like It
It's about the decor, ambiance and cocktails. I am not a fan of the nibble menu, so go to drink, but don't expect to really eat at HH.

SAT-SUN

Bazi Bierbrasserie

Southeast Map
1522 SE 32nd Ave.
(503) 234-8888
www.bazipdx.com

Happy Hours
3:00-7:00 pm and 10:00pm–close Daily
★All day Sunday

Food Deals $3.00-$8.00
Wide-ranging menu of more than a dozen items: kale chips, veggie and carnivorous burgers, croquettes, skewers, mac and cheese, salads, and seasonal house specialties.

Drink Specials
$1.00 off select beers; $5.00 wine; $3.50 wells
$5.00 cocktails (full bar including award-winning signature BEER cocktails!)

Atmosphere *The* place for Belgian beers on tap! They rotate 17 taps in all, fill growlers, and have over 50 bottles. Nice back bar area; lounge space with couches and tables up front. Roll-up garage door, lots of light, and several picnic tables outside. "A wine bar of beer."

Why I Really Like It
The bier! But the good food, too. Plus fun movie and TV nights. This would be my neighborhood go-to if I lived near here.

SAT-SUN

Bellino *New!*

~ 2016 ~ TOP 10 **Superstar**

GOLDEN TICKET!

Downtown (East)
1230 NW Hoyt
(503) 208-2992
www.bellinoportland.com

Happy Hours
4:00-6:00pm Daily

Food Deals 3
$4.00-$8.00
Tough decisions to be made! Unique, gourmet Sicilian dishes with Italian names: things like penne bolognese, stuffed eggplant, bruschetta, potato croquettes, busiati pasta, fried meatballs.

Drink Specials 3
$4.00 beer; $5.00 wines; $6.00 select cocktails (Each category offers a number of choices)

Atmosphere 3
This is the old Fratelli space. Quality interior design results in a very attractive, Pearlesque loft-style dinner space. Soft touches with thick tapestry curtains and antique frames balance artsy lead-pipe lighting and old woods.

New this Year/First Impressions
Excellent food, ambiance, Italian spirit and wine! One of those places where it's love at first bite. It's a whole new take on Italian cooking given the Sicilian slant to savoring. Try their Monday night feast for a real treat!

Benson/Palm Court

Downtown (East) Map
309 SW Broadway
(503) 228-2000
www.bensonhotel.com

Happy Hours
4:00–6:00pm and 9:00pm-close Daily

Food Deals 3
$2.00-$6.00
Well-priced, portioned, picked and plated: Varies somewhat seasonally with delicious items like oysters, soup, salads, fish & chips, calamari, and several sandwiches, and a big cheeseburger!

Drink Specials 3
$3.00 craft drafts; $5.00 wines; $6.00 cocktail

Atmosphere 3+
Historic and Fancy with a capital "F," their Palm Court Bar in the hotel lobby offers the opportunity to dine in high-style at a great value. It's simply fabulous, dahling! And whatever you do, never ever miss it at Christmas time!

Why I Really Like It
The Benson has serious jaw-dropping beauty inside and out! The lobby and open restaurant and bar in this historically distinctive and grand hotel are absolutely gorgeous! Great deals at Happy Hour, but dinner is awesome and a real value as well. Live jazz Wed-Sat!

Bent Brick

Pearl Map
1639 NW Marshall
(503) 688-1655
www.thebentbrick.com

Happy Hours
5:00–6:00pm Tues–Sun

Food Deals 3
$3.00-$7.00
Follows (and helps establish) the trending, funky-fresh, Northwest foodie thing: oysters on the half shell, seasonal soup, cheeses and hams, salads, Chicago-inspired hotdog.

Drink Specials 3
$4.00 drafts; $6.00 house wines
$5.00 select cocktails (old-fashioneds on tap!)

Atmosphere 3
Rustic and warm with brick walls (but of course) and an upscale angle on a neighborhood tavern. It's not a big place, and there's a well-designed waiting/lounge area at the entrance with a cool, artsy wooden "tree" to sit beneath. Park Kitchen chef/owner (and James Beard Award nominee).

Why I Really Like It
This one is in more for their general reputation. It's a bit light on heavy food for me, but so many others rave and praise!

SAT-SUN

Bit House Saloon

New!

Central Eastside
727 SE Grand Ave.
503-954-3913
www.bithousesaloon.com

Happy Hours
3:00-7:00pm Daily

Food Deals 2
$2.00-$9.00
Just a bit of saloon-style bites like potato chips, biscuits, beer nuts, fries, wings, bologna-wrapped stuffed jalapeños or a bologna sandwich.

Drink Specials 2
$1.00 off drafts; $6.00 wines; $6.00 rosés all day
$6.00 Moscow mules and fave house cocktails

Atmosphere 3
Nice work on a big remodel of East Bank Saloon! Giant space with several seating areas including an awesome beer garden with firepit out back. Historic building with gritty character but totally cozy. Brick walls, old captain chairs, chalkboard signs and antique lighting.

New this Year/First Impressions
Old-style Portland-y and a kind of step back in time, but still every bit up to current trends. Cool vibe and would work well for groups of all sizes. Killer cocktails! Already, it's an extremely popular newbie and I expect that to continue.

Bluehour

Pearl Map
250 NW 13th Ave.
(503) 226-3394
www.bluehouronline.com

Happy Hours
4:00–6:30pm Mon–Fri; 5:00-6:30pm Sat

Food Deals 3
$1.00–$7.00
Still keeping us happy after all these years with an always-impressive menu. Seasonal focus, with things like winter soups, summer salads, meat, cheese, fruit and/or nut plates, and a uniquely delicious Bluehour cheeseburger.

Drink Specials 3
$4.00 draft beers; $6.00 house wines
$20 select bottle wine; $6.00 specialty cocktails

Atmosphere 3+
Impressive lofted interior; very well-designed—a Portland standout! Trés trendy and active scene (can be a touch loud). Happy Hour sidewalk patio dining allowed—and totally enjoyed! Ultra cool lighting effects at night. LOVE it!

Why I Really Like It
Again, it's a solidly impressive Happy Hour, as all of owner Bruce Carey's places are (23 Hoyt, Clarklewis, Sauceboox). For a real treat, try a full dinner here!

SAT-SUN / ALL MON

Brix

Downtown (East) Map
1338 NW Hoyt
(503) 943-5995
www.brixtavern.com

Happy Hours
3:00–6:30pm and 9:30pm-close Daily
★All night Monday

Food Deals 3
$2.95-7.95
18 items with seasonal variations of meal-sized food: sliders, ribs, soups, salads, wings, yummy Brix chips, cheddar fries, burger, tacos, pizza.

Drink Specials 3
$1.00 off drafts (or try one of 30 cans of beer)
$1.00 off wine; $5.00 cocktails (nice, wide array)

Atmosphere 3
A popular and perfect sportsbar/restaurant/lounge in the Pearl. The front half is very social with brick walls, extra-long bar, and chalkboard menu. Back half hosts the dining crowd, though is also open for Happy Hourers. Plus, an elevated private loft space for groups. Sidewalk HH too.

Why I Really Like It
Big and versatile spot that has a nice, high-end American "barstaurant" appeal. Beautiful and spacious, but very comfortable and casual.

Café Castagna

Hawthorne (off map)
1752 SE Hawthorne
(503) 231-9959
www.castagnarestaurant.com

Happy Hours
5:00-6:00pm and 9:00pm-close Tues-Fri

Food Deals 3
$2.00–$8.00
Menu changes frequently, but hosts delicious and unique items like salmon tartine, seasonal soups, fresh salads, flatbreads, pastas, and be sure to try their famous burgers!

Drink Specials 3
$4.00 drafts; $5.00 wines and wells
$5.00 specialty cocktails (4)

Atmosphere 3
Contemporary simplicity with sleek lines, natural colors within a neutral color palette, and big front windows, which give this half of the restaurant more of a café feel. Cute little patio, too!

Why I Really Like It
Castagna Restaurant next door has totally epic food! It is noted in pretty much every Best-of List, and we get to sample just a small piece of the quality, care, and attention that goes into their cooking, but at Happy Hour. It's still night and day difference, but so is the price!

Café Nell

NW/Nob Hill Map
1987 NW Kearney
(503) 295-6487
www.cafenell.com

Happy Hours
3:00–6:00pm Mon-Fri ★All night Wed
4:00-6:00pm Sat

Food Deals 3
$2.00–$8.00
Diverse menu with seasonal spins and items like soups, salad, oysters, mac & cheese, tacos, clams, flatbreads, walnuts, or daily pasta.

Drink Specials 3
$1.00 off drafts; $5.00 wine; $5.00 bubbles or champagne cocktails; $5.50 martinis/cocktails

Atmosphere 3
Cute, little hidden gem tucked away on a quiet tree-lined street. A welcoming brasserie both day and night. Tiny Parisian-style bar with big cushy couch and cafe windows opening to the outside.

Why I Really Like It
The kind of place you could stay all day into the night! Changes with the light and crowd. Always feels so welcoming.

SAT-SUN

Casa del Matador

NW/Nob Hill Map
1438 NW 23rd Ave.; (503) 228-2855
Lloyd Center Map
2424 East Burnside; (503) 719-5757
www.matadorrestaurants.com

Happy Hours
4:00–6:00pm & 10:00pm-close Daily

Food Deals 3
$5.00-$6.00
Four kinds of quesadillas, choice of six tacos, and even more: nachos, habanero or garlic prawns; soups, chili, salad, spicy wings, or calamari.

Drink Specials 0
No drink specials, but know that they have over 130 varieties of tequila!

Atmosphere 3
A handsome and sexy interior worthy of the title "Matador" greets you upon entering! Stunning, wrought iron artistry, gilded mirrors and rustic stucco walls. A stand-out space with compelling, centrally located, circular fireplace.

Why I Really Like It
I love it for the food and ambiance, though also always long for drink deals. Years later, they still really pack 'em in, so I don't see that wish coming true too soon. Still love it though!

SAT-SUN

Ciao Vito

Alberta Map
2203 NE Alberta
(503) 282-5522
www.ciaovito.net

Happy Hours
4:30–7:00pm Sun-Thur; 4:30-6:30pm Fri-Sat

Food Deals 3
$4.00–$9.00
Wow! Giant array of 15 or so seasonal, mostly Spanish-influenced menu items: salumi plate, grilled octopus, spaghettis, salads, spicy prawns, meatballs, polenta, sausage or pork dishes.

Drink Specials 2
Random beer specials; $5.00 wines

Atmosphere 3
Classic elegance with warmth and style, nice neighborhood welcoming feel with bright and funky mural on outside side wall.

Why I Really Like It
Good food that changes enough to keep things interesting, but keeps to a number of basics I know I'll love. One of funky Alberta Street's nicest places.

Cibo

Southeast Map
3593 SE Division
(503) 719-5377
www.cibopdx.com

Happy Hours
5:00-6:00pm Daily (from 4:00 Fri-Sun)
9:00-10:00pm Sun-Wed; 10:00-11:00pm Fri-Sat

Food Deals 3
$3.00-$8.00
Delicious wood-fired pizzas, paninis, polenta, fries, spaghetti, wings, rings, burgers.

Drink Specials 3
$4.00 drafts; $5.00 wine; $4.00 wells
$6.00-7.00 rotating specialty cocktails

Atmosphere 3
Pronounced CHEE-bo. Neighborhood bar from the owner of Basta's, but the casual bar vibe is a disconnect from the fancy food served. Tables and booths line the slatted wood walls, all surrounding the giant central bar/kitchen that the whole place revolves around.

Why I Really Like It
It's a good mix between a restaurant and a bar, and has a big local fan base that keeps the place bustling. The big open kitchen and bar activity in the middle is always interesting, and you get to cut your pizza with scissors.

Cellar 55 Tasting Room

Vancouver
1812 Washington
(360) 693-2700
www.cellar55tastingroom.com

Happy Hours
2:00-6:00pm Wed; 2:00-8:00pm Thurs
2:00-6:00pm Fri; 2:00-6:00pm Sun

Food Deals 2
$1.00-$4.00 off meat & cheese plates

Drink Specials 2
$1.00-$3.00 off glasses of wine

Atmosphere 3
A favorite for all of Vancouver. Chill wine bar / tasting room / co-op featuring boutique wineries from Walla Walla and Eastern WA. Fun, large, laid-back room with live music on most weekends; sometimes outside in the wine garden area. Brick walls with wine barrel tables and comfy couches.

Why I Really Like It
It's a great place to hang out! There's a nice little community of friendly wine drinkers here. Plus, the Wine Storage part of this place stores your wine at a perfect cellar temperature of 55 degrees, and monthly membership includes not only a locker, but also use of their private party room.

SAT-SUN

Chez Machin

Southeast Map
3553 SE Hawthorne
(503) 736-9381
www.chezmachin.com

Happy Hours
3:00–6:00pm Daily

Food Deals 3
$3.00-$6.00
Ooh-la-la! A recently updated Happy Hour, and better than ever: French onion soup, escargot, cheese and fruit plate, crepes (ham & cheese, tomato & mozzarella, sweet/Nutella), salads.

Drink Specials 2
$1.00 off all beer, cider, wine and mimosas
$5.00 off all bottles of wine

Atmosphere 3
Trés cute!!! Dripping with charm like a good creperie should be, with a nice little patio, too. Great crepes. Switched hands in 2014 to the very capable, former owner of Vinideus.

Why I Really Like It
High cuteness factor, especially when it's dark outside, and with some imagination activation, you can feel like you're on a vacation in Paris. More casual than fancy, and easy on the wallet.

Circa 33

Southeast Map
3348 SE Belmont Ave
(503) 477-7682
www.circa33bar.com

Happy Hours
4:00–6:00pm Daily; ★All night Monday
11:00–6:00pm Sat-Sun

Food Deals 2
$4.00–$6.50
Bar menu with slight tasty twists on basics with seasonal variations: burger, fries, calamari, mac & cheese, sliders, salad, flautas, fish & chips.

Drink Specials 3
$1.00 off drafts; $5.50 house wine
$4.00 wells; $6.00 planter's punch

Atmosphere 3
Around about the 33rd block, so you'll always remember where it is, and also relates to 1933, the year Prohibition was repealed. It's true to theme and concept, and exudes a genuine character. Best at night!

Why I Really Like It
Fun speakeasy vibe. Love the alleyway patio – and the secret cocktail club that's hidden behind a bookcase! The red light outside the building means it's open. Blue means it's closed.

Clarklewis

Central Eastside Map
1001 SE Water Ave.
(503) 235-2294
www.clarklewispdx.com

Happy Hours
4:30–6:30pm Mon–Fri

Food Deals 3
$1.00–$7.00
Menu changes often, with about a dozen or so chef's choice nibbles like seasonal salads or soups, bread, cheese, nuts, mac & cheese, seared lamb loin, or a special cheeseburger.

Drink Specials 3
$5.00 select beer; $6.00 wine; $6.00 bubbles
$5.00 martini or gimlet

Atmosphere 3
Sophisticated renovation of old loading dock with northwest and industrial-chic stylings; full, long wall of streetscape gridded windows (open or candlelit), big wooden tables for groups and tucked-away two-tops. A perfect date place!

Why I Really Like It
Yep – another awesome Happy Hour from the owner with a magic touch, Bruce Carey (23 Hoyt, Bluehour, Saucebox).

SAT-SUN

Clyde Common

Downtown (West) Map
1014 SW Stark
(503) 228-3333
www.clydecommon.com

Happy Hours
3:00–6:00pm Daily

Food Deals 3
$3.00–$6.00
A front-runner in serving alternative dishes with a number of quality restaurants following suit. Always a unique Happy Hour menu with about a dozen often "weird" menu items like grilled duck hearts, kielbasa, sweet & sour pork, pickles & pate, chicken liver mousse, saganaki, or mussels.

Drink Specials 3
$4.00 drafts; $6.00 select wines
$6.00 award-winning cocktails

Atmosphere 3
Big, open warehouse space like an unfinished, art school gallery. Rough wood floors, banged-up bar stools, stenciled signage, and butcher paper walls give it a working-man edge. Popular social scene with community table seating.

Why I Really Like It
Popcorn and cocktail experts. *The* place to take friends from out of town. Near Living Room Theater. Pssst.... Ask about the speakeasy downstairs!

DarSalam

SAT

New!

GOLDEN TICKET!

Downtown (East) Map
320 SW Alder; (503) 444-7813
Alberta Map
2921 NE Alberta; (503) 206-6148
www.darsalamportland.com

Happy Hours
4:00–6:00pm Mon-Fri; Sat 2:00-5:00pm Alder

Food Deals 3 $2.00-$10.00
Delicious Iraqi sides include a beautiful beet salad (a must!), pickled mango salad, hummus, baba ganoush, or tahziki; homemade soups, green salad, mezza platters, chicken or lamb shawarma. Gluten-free flatbread option!

Drink Specials 2
$1.00 off beer; $2.00 off wine

Atmosphere 3
Second downtown location has show-stopping mural/tile work that makes it look like a royal palace fancily done up in royal blues and golds. The original Alberta location is in a sweet, little turquoise home with a cozy interior. Golden walls are adorned on every square inch with photos, mirrors and Iraqi art.

New this Year/First Impressions
The food! The people! Translation is "House of Peace." Ask them about the owner's love story :-)

Departure

Downtown (East) Map
525 SW Morrison; Rooftop
(503) 222-9996
www.departureportland.com

Happy Hours
4:00–6:00pm Mon–Sat

Food Deals 3+
$3.00–$9.00
Giant, mostly Asian-inspired menu with things like maki rolls, edamame, wings, skewers, salads, udon noodles, fried rice, wings, and much more!

Drink Specials 3
$5.00 beer; $6.00 wine; $6.00 sake of the day

Atmosphere 3+
It's a departure from Portland norm in every way! From the funky elevator entrance and Space-Mountain-style exit, you know you're someplace different. Warm weather offers three top-floor patio seating areas with stellar views of the city below and mountains in the distance. Website has spectacular photography for a pre-tour.

Why I Really Like It
Because it's awesome! See all the reasons above. This place is also a Top 10 Happy Hour :-)

Dragonwell

Downtown (East) Map
735 SW First Ave.
(503) 224-0800
www.dragonwellbistro.com

Happy Hours
3:00–6:30pm Mon–Fri (until 6pm Fri)
9:30–10:30pm Fri–Sat

Food Deals 3+
$1.00–$6.00
Phenomenal food! And 25+ choices! Amazing line-up of *everything:* General Tso's, orange or sesame chicken; several versions of fried rice, lo mein, or salt & pepper dishes; several kinds of noodle dishes; salad or spring rolls, and more!

Drink Specials 3
$2.00 Sapporo; $5.00 red and white wine
$5.00 Happy Sake or Cocktail of the Day

Atmosphere 3
Serene, upscale restaurant with a wonderful mix of understated elegance, Asian simplicity and exceptional design. Bright by day, dark and intimate by night. Flexible group seating.

Why I Really Like It
The giant array of Happy Hour food choices, and the deliciousness of it, too! Nice interior.

SAT-SUN

Driftwood Room

Downtown (West) Map
729 SW 15th Ave.
(503) 223-6311
www.hoteldeluxeportland.com

Happy Hours
★2:00–6:30pm and 9:30pm–close Daily

Food Deals 3
$4.00–$8.00
Outstanding menu with two dozen choices! Mac & cheese, portobello mushroom burger, BBQ ribs, Oregon cheeseburgers, sizzling forest mushrooms, flatbread, salads, selection of fries, and much more!

Drink Specials 2
$5.00 daily draft; $7.00 wines
$25.00 bottle of wine (red or white)
$7.00 champagne cocktails

Atmosphere 3+
Off the very impressive grand lobby of the Hotel deLuxe, the Driftwood has a dark, discreet, and fancy ratpack appeal in a kidney-shaped, dimly-lit, wooden room with NW touches. LOVE it!

Why I Really Like It
It's a classic! You can also sit over in Gracie's at Happy Hour as they take overflow from the crowds. Gracie's is bright and beautiful by day and fabulous and fancy by night.

East India Company

Downtown (West) Map
821 SW 11th Ave.
(503) 227-8815
www.eastindiacopdx.com

Happy Hours
5:00–7:00pm Mon–Sat

Food Deals 3
$3.00–$6.00
Expanded menu with old favorites and several new ones: eggplant dip, wings, fish fingerlings, veggie fritters, croquettes, spicy peanuts, lamb slider, fritters, or garbanzo bean salad.

Drink Specials 3
$4.00 drafts; $4.00-5.00 house wine
$1.00 off all drinks; $5.00-6.95 cocktails

Atmosphere 2
Nice enough overall, but the front bar decor and ambiance at Happy Hour pales in comparison to the dark, rich, romantic restaurant in back. But if you get a group of 6-8 together and call ahead, you can get a nice table in the restaurant with the Happy Hour menu. Otherwise, tables are made for 2-3 people up front in the bar.

Why I Really Like It
One of the very few Indian restaurants that does Happy Hour! And it's a nice, upscale place.

Ecliptic Brewing

North/NE Map
825 N Cook
(503) 265-8002
www.eclipticbrewing.com

Hoppy Hours
3:00–6:00pm Daily

Food Deals 3
$2.00–$10.00
A step up from typical pub menus with great food including seasonal changes: burgers, salads, drumsticks, daily soup, fried russets.

Drink Specials 2
$1.00 off drafts and house cocktails

Atmosphere 3
It's an epic approach to Ecliptic's giant cement building that houses both its brewing facilities and their cool and comfortable restaurant. Named for the yearly path around the sun, with interesting sparks of celestial designs. Great place! Big menu with great food and beer. Outside seating on patio.

Why I Really Like It
I think this would be my favorite Brewery Happy Hour. The food is up a notch from the usual brewery pub quality. And I like the beer :-)

ALL SUN

El Gaucho

Downtown (East) Map
319 SW Broadway
(503) 227-8794
www.elgaucho.com

Happy Hours
4:30–6:00pm Mon–Fri; 10:00pm–close Mon-Sat
★4:30pm-close Sun

Food Deals 3
$6.00–$18.00
Eight great menu items – on the spendy side, but marked down from regular menu: steak frites, cheddar bacon burger, beef sliders, ribs, sautéed tenderloin tips, fish & chips, salad,

Drink Specials 3
$4.00 select beer; $7.00 red or white wine
$7.00 cocktails (four)

Atmosphere 3
Notably classy, classic steakhouse. Enjoy a memorable evening in their dramatic lounge. See a celebrity or just feel like one yourself. (Author note: I think they have the best steaks in the city! Worth the occasional splurge.)

Why I Really Like It
It just feels so fancy! At Happy Hour you really do get a taste of what its like to dine there. Mouth-watering steak and impeccable service.

Eleni's Philoxenia

Pearl Map
112 NW 9th Ave.
(503) 227-2158
www.elenisrestaurant.com

Happy Hours
5:00–6:30pm Sun-Fri and 8:30-9:30pm Tues-Fri

Food Deals 3
$6.00-$8.00
Big delicious portions and I always want all of it! Several unique and healthy salad options, Greek meatballs, pita with your choice of four dips, clams & mussels, and the BEST grilled calamari!

Drink Specials 2
$4.00 drafts; $6.00 house wine

Atmosphere 3
A beautiful, fine-dining restaurant with white linen tablecloths, deep rich woods, and white swags that soften the ceiling. Their name translates to "hospitality," and although you'll get to dine in fanciness at Happy Hour, you'll feel right at home, relaxed, and welcomed.

Why I Really Like It
Amazingly under the radar, somehow this one escaped even me until last year, and it was at once an immediate favorite! *The* best place for Greek food in Portland, hands down.

Elephant's Deli

NW/Nob Hill Map
115 NW 22nd Ave.
(503) 299-6304
www.elephantsdeli.com

Happy Hours
3:00–6:00pm Daily

Food Deals 3
$4.00-$6.00
They've really stepped up their menu from recent years! Beef, pork, or bean sliders, fondue, cheeses, chicken tacos, fries, calamari, pizza. A whole artisan deli/bakery with desserts too!

Drink Specials 3
$4.00 drafts, $5.00 wines, $5.00-$7.00 cocktails

Atmosphere 3
It's a super-cute, little urban bar tucked inside a quaint, but modern, country store. Eat and shop, drink and bring home good wine, and grab gourmet to go! Fun outdoor deck, too.

Why I Really Like It
It's really quite a unique place for Happy Hour! I really haven't seen the likes of it anywhere else. Cuteness!

Epif Pisco Lounge

North/NE Map
404 NE 28th Ave.
(971) 254-8680
www.epifpdx.com

Happy Hours
4:00–6:00pm Wed-Sun

Food Deals 0
No discounts at this point, but they are brand-spanking new and seeing how things go. Expect deals later – check their website. Vegetarians may well love this place, others may find the food somewhat odd. We'll see what HH brings.

Drink Specials 2
$4.00 drafts; $6.00 wine; $5.00-$6.00 piscos

Atmosphere 2
Bright aqua restaurant with food, piscos, and interior and exterior design inspired by the Andes Region of South America. Exterior rooftop is built around a tree! Interior uses old church pews, gym bleachers, and tables brought by the owners all the way from Chile.

New this Year/First Impressions
Still too new to judge. They didn't go too wild in decorating the place. Needs some warming up, and some marketing help.

Equinox

North/NE Map
830 N Shaver St
(503) 460-3333
www.equinoxrestaurantpdx.com

Happy Hours
4:00–6:00pm Mon–Fri

Food Deals 3
$3.00–$6.00
Menu with about a dozen exceptionally delicious items! Varies a bit with the seasons with unique items like crepes, roasted beets, salad, mussels, calamari, soup, fries, spaetzle, or cheeseburger.

Drink Specials 3
$4.00 drafts; $5.00 wine; $4.00 wells
$5.50 specialty cocktails

Atmosphere 3
Enter through their delightful front patio (where you can enjoy Happy Hour, weather permitting). Inside, it's warm and woody throughout with old, rough wood floors, natural wood tables, and paneled half-walls. Skylight and garage door.

Why I Really Like It
It's off the radar being around the corner, off the busy street, but my big go-to in the Mississippi area. Mostly for the food, but also for the patio.

Farm Café

Central East Side Map
10 SE 7th Ave
(503) 736-3276
www.thefarmcafe.com

Happy Hours
5:00–6:00pm Mon–Fri

Food Deals 3
$2.00–$6.00
Short but sweet menu – fresh goodies change with the seasons, and even daily: hummus plate, arancini, crostini, pickle plate, salads, soup.

Drink Specials 2
$1.00 off draft beer; $5.00 red and white wines
$5.00 choice cocktails

Atmosphere 3
High-level cuteness alert! Located in a renovated, old Victorian home dripping with charm. Romantic and intimate with several meandering, cozy dining rooms. Big seasonal patio and back bar.

Why I Really Like It
Charming! And good. I don't hear about it being touted enough, although it should be frequently mentioned as a top choice. Perfect date place.

The Fields

Pearl Map
1139 NW 11th Ave.
(503) 841-6601
www.thefieldspdx.com

Happy Hours
3:00-6:00pm Mon-Fri and 10:00pm-close Daily

Food Deals 3
$4.00-$7.00
Exceptionally delicious bar eats, and lots of them! And what's already putting them on the map is their soon-to-be-world-famous avocado fries! Plus nachos, poutine, salads, burgers, wings, sliders, and creatively-stacked polenta fries.

Drink Specials 3
$4.00 drafts; $5.00 house wines
$5.00 wells; $7.00 house cocktails

Atmosphere 3
I just love it when a place hits it out of the park! The Fields Bar & Grill has nailed that elusive mix of a sports bar plus comfort with upscale design, all with maximum TV viewing and excellent food. Outside patio, too! Former Metrovino space.

Why I Really Like It
It keeps the boyfriend happy with plenty of TVs around, and I get the bonus of a nice place with good food – including some healthy options which are rarely seen at a typical sports bar.

Firehouse

North/NE (off map)
711 NE Dekum
(503) 954-1702
www.firehousepdx.com

Happy Hours
5:00–6:00pm Daily

Food Deals 3
$3.00–$11.00
Delicious but limited and somewhat pricey menu. Items like a roasted beet salad, wood-fired pizza, meatballs, and fried cauliflower. They grow herbs and veggies in their own garden!

Drink Specials 2
$4.00 drafts; $6.00 wines; $6.00 daily cocktail

Atmosphere 3
A very cool building from the outside and in, and on its own triangular block. Firehouse 29 from the early 1900s has been renovated with lots of sweat and dreams and now houses one of the city's cutest Happy Hour places. Open seating everywhere, including their smokin' patio!

Why I Really Like It
It smells great from the moment you step in. Cozy inside and lovely outside.

SAT-SUN

Gold Dust Meridian

Southeast Map
3267 SE Hawthorne
(503) 239-1143
www.golddustmeridian.com

Happy Hours
★2:00–8:00pm Daily

Food Deals 2
$4.00–$6.00
Huge menu of 16 items follows period style and includes deviled eggs, grilled cheese trio (served with soup and salad), Caesar, ravioli, stuffed mushrooms, mac & cheese, wings, dip, ceviche.

Drink Specials 2
.50 cents off pints & wells; $1.00 off wine

Atmosphere 3
Marathon Happy Hour joint with a super dark interior that is steeped deep in authentic retro charm and is at once swanky, chill, and ultra-cool. Fun side patio for an entirely different experience.

Why I Really Like It
It's a step back in time, yet a mod-trendy-hipster mecca. All in all, a six hour Happy Hour makes it a total *golden* favorite!

Grant House

Vancouver
1101 Officer's Row
(360) 906-1101
www.thegranthouse.us

Happy Hours
3:00–6:00pm Tues–Sat

Food Deals 3
$1.00-$9.00
Enjoy high-end restaurant quality food and ambiance! Big menu: fish tacos, salad, burgers, fries, prawns, hummus plate, flat bread.

Drink Specials 2
$4.00 drafts; $5.00 wines

Atmosphere 3
Inside the grounds of historic Fort Vancouver. Charming, turn-of-the-century estate (Ulysses S. Grant lived here in the 1850s). A perfect blend of class and coziness inside and out. Gorgeous patio! Worth a trip if need be. It always feels like you've stepped into vacation mode here.

Why I Really Like It
On a cold rainy day, you can shake off the chill and quietly enjoy a roaring fire. Or on a perfectly sunny afternoon, bask in peace on the lovely patio that overlooks the back garden. And wait... what?! This is Vancouver?!

ALL SAT / ALL SUN

High Noon

Downtown (East)
823 SW 2nd Ave.
(503) 841-6411
www.highnoonpdx.com

Happy Hours
2:00–6:00pm and 9:00pm–close Daily
★3:00pm-close Sat–Sun

Food Deals 3
$3.00-$6.00
Ooh! Mix and match your frybread, corn cake, or salad to top with brisket, chicken, pork or veggies, add tasty toppings (chilies, jack cheese, pickled red onion, cilantro, pico de gallo), and creamy tomatillo or roasted green chile dressings.

Drink Specials 2
$1.00 off beer, wine and house cocktails
$8.00 featured tequila cocktails (Margarita, Mezcal Mule or a Bloody Maria)

Atmosphere 3
Cool space! On the edgy side decor-wise for a downtown location, but makes it quirky and casual. It's a new quick-serve-with-cocktail-bar concept from the folks behind Barlow and Picnic House. Unique Wild West "High Noon" graphics.

New this Year/First Impressions
I really like the design sense of this restaurant group! And I love the long Sat-Sun HH hours!

Hokusei Sushi

Southeast Map
4246 SE Belmont
(971) 279-2161
www.hokuseisushi.com

Happy Hours
5:00-6:00pm Wed-Sun ★ All night Monday

Food Deals 3
$2.00–$6.00
Exceptional sushi here, and a big menu, but prices are all over the board, and (relatively) not much of it discounted for Happy Hour. Eight fun-to-pronounce menu items like wakame salad, edamame, tatsuta age, harumaki, gyu tan yaki.

Drink Specials 2
$1.00 off drafts and sake (half-off small hot sake)
$5.00 Happy Hour cocktail

Atmosphere 3
Serene, simple, and stark space. Contemporary design with clean lines, natural woods, open-air garage door wall, and cement floors. Super-long group table, pretty artwork, and sushi bar seating.

Why I Really Like It
Awesome food!

SAT-SUN

Hop City Tavern

New!

Downtown (East)
921 SW 6th Ave.
(503) 220-2685
www.hopcitytavern.com

Happy Hours
4:00-6:00pm Daily

Food Deals 3 $3.00-$7.00
Gastropub food highlighting Portland-style food (complete with local sourcing) and putting a new spin on basics like a BLT with arugula and tomato jam, wings with a spicy cherry BBQ sauce, mac & cheese made with HUB beer, bacon-wrapped dates, flatbread, pretzels, fried pickles, mussels.

Drink Specials 3
$4.00 draft pints; $5.00 wine: $6.00 wells

Atmosphere 2
A giant improvement and totally new look from the former Bistro 921 space! It almost floats and glows in clean, modern white compared to the traditional, dark look of the Hilton lobby that the space pretty much shares. The overall experience would change depending on the convention in town and the surrounding activities, or lack thereof.

New this Year/First Impressions
It seems pretty touristy... some hotel bars can get away with that, but you're practically sitting in the lobby. And it doesn't match the hotel decor at all so it's an awkward space.

SAT-SUN/ALL MON

Iconic

North/NE Map
2226 NE Broadway
(503) 946-1621
www.iconiclounge.com

Happy Hours
3:30–6:30pm Daily; ★All day Monday

Food Deals 3
$3.99–$5.99
Huge portions of many beloved basics, but with a jazzy twist. I deem their "Iconic Mac" the best mac & cheese in town! A dozen items overall: cauliflower romesco, honey ginger green beans, sweet potato tots, spinach and artichoke pizza, Elvis fries, pickled pepper poppers, and more!

Drink Specials 3
$3.00 cheap or $4.00 trendy beer; $5.00 or $8.00 wines (5 oz. or 8 oz. pours), $6.00 cocktail

Atmosphere 3
Giant photos of iconic legends of the silver screen adorn the deep red and gray walls. Big screen TV plays old movie classics. Signature cocktails named after movie stars and movie titles. Perfection!

Why I Really Like It
High points across the board, which isn't easy for a "bar" to get. Good variety of good food, and fun movies always playing in the background.

SAT-SUN

Imperial

Downtown (East) Map
410 SW Broadway
(503) 228-7222
www.imperialpdx.com

Happy Hours
2:00–6:00pm Daily

Food Deals 3
$3.00–$10.00
Ever changing menu with one of Portland's best burgers! Nice mix of some basics and random things you won't see on other menus: fries, fried pig's tail, meat and cheese plates, smoked tongue sliders, oysters, salad, chicken liver pate.

Drink Specials 3
$5.00 select imperial pints; $8.00 wines
$5.00 cocktails (choice of two)

Atmosphere 3
Quality restaurant in Hotel Lucia brought to us by Vitaly Paley (Paley's Place). The talk of the town upon opening, and awarded Willamette Week's Restaurant of the Year 2015! Loft style with cement beams, wood floors, and brick-like tiles in browns and tans. Unique wallpaper. Popular!

Why I Really Like It
It's a Portland-perfect cocktail bar, and one of our very best restaurants for real dining.

Interurban

North/NE Map
4057 N Mississippi
(503) 284-6669
www.interurbanpdx.com

Happy Hours
3:00–6:00pm Mon–Fri; 10:00pm–close Sunday

Food Deals 3
$2.00–$7.00
Tavern sugo, soup, wings, chili dog, salad, chili quesadilla, pups & frites, grilled broccolini, wings, salads, and hot oatmeal cookies.

Drink Specials 3
$2.00 mini beers; $4.00 jumbo cask draft
$5.00 house wines; $5.00 bubbly cocktails
Plus deals on rotating taster shots of the week

Atmosphere 3
This "publican's table" gives us an urban, industrial hideaway with cozy neighborhood charm (albeit a bit loud with the crowd). Long, front bar area with a modern-day speakeasy upstairs. Popular and big back patio.

Why I Really Like It
It's one of our "old-standbys" in this area. Cool and casual with a nice back deck.

SAT-SUN

Irving St. Kitchen

Pearl Map
703 NW 13th Ave.
(503) 343-9440
www.irvingstreetkitchen.com

Happy Hours
4:30–6:00pm Daily

Food Deals 3
$5.00–$6.00
Unique menu items totally matching the theme. Seasonal salad, Cajun fries, jambalaya, chicken-fried oysters, meatballs, chicken wings, tots.

Drink Specials 3
$3.00 tall boy (with $3.00 whiskey back)
$6.00 house wines; $6.00 specialty cocktails

Atmosphere 3
Trendy and rustic with TONS of character and attention to design details. Very popular, front and center bar with seating all around. Lots of nice little nooks and separate seating areas throughout.

Why I Really Like It
I'm always noting the creative little touches that are everywhere in the interior design here. A highly-praised chef and great food. I always yearn for more options at Happy Hour though.

Island Cafe

Columbia River
250 NE Tomahawk Island Drive
(503) 283-0362
www.islandcafepdx.com

Happy Hours
3:00-6:00pm Mon-Fri (Mid-April thru mid-Oct)

Food Deals
$2.95-$5.95
Pub grub perfect for pirates and parrotheads: quesadilla, spicy wings, chicken skewers, fries, burgers, popcorn shrimp, pork sliders, hummus.

Drink Specials
$4.00 drafts; $5.00 wine, wells, beach drinks

Atmosphere+
Have you ever wondered which place is my *super-secret* favorite bar ever? I've kinda kept it a hidden treasure... until now. Located down a steep dock in a particular harbor up north, is the Island Cafe. My favorite place in Portland! Totally tropical! Happy Hour here is a magic kind of medicine, and my "magic points" are big for this place. When visiting, be sure to stop at my **Happy Mermaid Gift Shop/Gallery** next door!

Why I Really Like It
I love it!!! I bought my Gift Shop to enjoy all my days down on the water here! It's joyful vacation attitude all the time.

Jake's Famous Crawfish

SAT-SUN

Downtown (West) Map
401 SW 12th Ave.
(503) 226-1419
www.jakesfamouscrawfish.com

Happy Hours
3:00–6:00pm Daily; 9:00-11:00pm Sun–Thurs
10:00pm–midnight Fri–Sat

Food Deals 3+
$2.95–$5.95
17 items and outstanding, hearty sizes: Enjoy the ever-famous $3.95 cheeseburger with fries, chicken sandwich, fish tacos, calamari, gumbo, sushi rolls, salmon cake, wings, mussels, shrimp.

Drink Specials 0
Sadly, no drink deals

Atmosphere 3
Old-school fun with traditional class; outdoor sidewalk dining. Considered one of the top seafood restaurants in the nation, Jake's has been a downtown landmark for more than 110 years. Location not to be confused with Jake's Grill (see next page).

Why I Really Like It
They really know what they're doing here. You can't not like Jake's! Either of them.

SAT / ALL SUN

Jake's Grill

Downtown (West) Map
611 SW 10th Ave.
(503) 220-1850
www.jakesgrill.com

Happy Hours
3:00–6:00pm Mon–Fri; 9:00pm–close Daily
★1:00–4:00pm Saturday; ★3:00pm–close Sun

Food Deals 3+
$2.95–$5.95
Changing menu of 12 items with outstanding, hearty sizes: wings, cheeseburger with fries, ribs, hummus, salmon taco, oyster shooters, flatbreads, pork tostada, crab & lobster croquette.

Drink Specials 3
$4.00 drafts; $6.00 red or white wine; $4.00 wells

Atmosphere 3
Stately and traditional with convivial class; fancy, white jacket and bowtie servers; connected with impressive Sentinel Hotel. Wildly popular and like Jake's Famous, pretty much always packed.

Why I Really Like It
This Jake's has drink deals! And weekend Happy Hours! It's also evey bit as crowded on weekdays. Try and go early.

Jantzen Beach Bar&Grill

Columbia River
909 N Hayden Island Drive
(503) 283-4466
www.redlionontheriver.com

Happy Hours
3:00–6:00pm Daily

Food Deals 2
$2.00–$10.00
About $2.00 off select appetizers: items like crostini, burgers, calamari, hummus, artichoke spinach dip, clams, beef skewers, tarts.

Drink Specials 3
$1.00 off drafts; $5.00 wines
$4.00 wells and martinis; $2.00 off cocktail list

Atmosphere 3
Wall-to-wall windows frame excellent river views! Large black & white photos reveal scenes of bygone glory days of Jantzen Beach Amusement Park. Enjoy Happy Hour seating anywhere in the understated, fine-dining restaurant or out on the long, outdoor patio. Fully remodeled and nicely appointed.

Why I Really Like It
On the waterfront. Gorgeous views with outside, elevated deck seating.

Karam Lebanese

Downtown (East) Map
515 SW 4th Ave.
(503) 223-0830
www.karamrestaurant.com

Happy Hours
2:00–6:00pm Mon–Fri

Food Deals 3+
$2.95
Deals on the basics and some mysteries: falafel, hummus, baleela (ultra-yummy, warmed, almost fluffy hummus), the best taboule, feta, fries, veggie kibbee nayee, arnabeet mekle, kafta.

Drink Specials 3
$3.00 select beer; $4.00 red or white wine

Atmosphere 3
They've relocated into a new space right near the old one, closer to Pioneer Place. Soaring ceiling covers a long and narrow dining room. Nice mix of old and new, perfectly reflecting Syrian and Lebanese roots with giant pillars, faux painting techniques covering the walls, and collections of hanging lanterns and lights.

Why I Really Like It
The food is delicious and inexpensive enough to get a bunch of everything and share. Great deals on drinks to boot. Super nice people too!

La Calaca Comelona

Southeast Map
2304 SE Belmont
(503) 239-9675
www.lacalacacomelona.com

A PERFECT 10
10 YEARS
– and counting –

GOLDEN TICKET!

Happy Hours
4:00-6:00pm
and 8:00pm-close Mon–Sat

Food Deals 3+
$2.75–$6.50
Authentic, truly delicious Mexican food! Pork and pineapple tacos (plus other varieties), salads, spicy potatoes, mini quesadillas, taquitos.

Drink Specials 3
50 cents off beer; $5.00 wines; $4.00 wells
$4.50 Margaritas and other bartender specials

Atmosphere 3+
Take a Mexican vacation to this Day-of-the-Dead-inspired taverna named "The Hungry Skeleton." Bright colorful walls, Mexican-style folk art at every glimpse and turn, and you can sit anywhere in the whole loco restaurant. Patio out back, but for dinner only.

Why I Really Like It
Excellent food with a great variety of choices. It's really hard to decide what to get here, but keep in mind that you can't make a wrong choice, and you can come back.

Lapellah

Vancouver
2520 Columbia House Blvd.
(360) 828-7911
www.lapellah.com

Happy Hours
3:30-6:00pm Daily / 9:00-11:00pm Fri-Sat

Food Deals 3 $2.00–$7.00
Big menu! Delicious and gourmet spins on classics with seasonal variations: burger, mac & cheese, wings, calamari, daily flat bread, salad, soup, olives, tacos, sliders, fries, and bacon-wrapped jalapenos.

Drink Specials 3
$3.50 drafts; $5.50 house wines or sangria
$4.00 wells and $5.50 specialty cocktails

Atmosphere 3
Northwest-style, natural and woody inside. Urban, rustic, loft-style interior with lots of slats of wood and a cool wall of glass plates in panes. Central and long group table dominates surrounding upolstered booths. Cool lighting. Patio seating. Same owners as **Roots** (also with a great Happy Hour, located at 19215 SE 34th Street; Camas).

Why I really like it
It's all about the food – and wood-fired ovens!

Las Primas

SAT-SUN

North/NE Map
3971 N Williams Ave, #103
(503) 206-5790
www.lasprimaskitchen.com

GOLDEN TICKET!

Happy Hours
3:00–6:00pm Tues–Sun

Food Deals 3
$2.50–$6.00
Delicious, unique food! Flavorful, classic sandwiches (pepper-rubbed pork, house-made sausage, or veggie), soup, empanadas, salads, – and chorizo saucy fries!

Drink Specials 3
$2.50-$4.00 beer; $4.00 wine; $4.00 sangría
$4.50 Inca borrachos
$6.00 pisco sours – choice of six!

Atmosphere 2
Simple restaurant with colorful, hand-painted welcome mural and Peruvian folk art pieces adorning white walls. Patterned after typical Lima-style sandwich shops with open kitchen, counter service and cement floors.

Why I really like it
Lots of flavors going on, and it's all so good! Bring a friend to share so you can get the fries
:-)

SAT / SUN & ALL MON

Lechon

~ 2016 ~
TOP 10
Superstar

New!

Downtown (East)
113 SW Naito Pkwy
(503) 219-9000
www.lechonpdx.com

Happy Hours
3:00-6:00pm and 9:00pm-close Daily
★All Night Monday

Food Deals 3 $3.00-$7.00
Love at first bite! Even before that as everything is plated beautifully! Lots to choose from with a talented, caring chef skillfully throwing down Argentinian and Chilean specialties like ceviche, empanadas, forest mushrooms, salad, stew, yuca chips, burgers, mussels, and *much* more.

Drink Specials 3
$4.00 beer; $6.00 wine; $4.00 wells
$6.00-$7.00 specialty cocktails

Atmosphere 3
Very cool space in an old, historic building across from the waterfront park just south of the Saturday Market. Stately, giant arched windows, exposed brick walls, and two huge fish and jellyfish tanks.

New this Year/First Impressions
Every once in a while, a place comes along and really knocks my socks off. Lechon is one of those places, and I am so excited about it!!!!

Levant

Lloyd Center-ish Map
2448 E Burnside
(503) 954-2322
www.levantpdx.com

Happy Hours
5:00-6:00pm and 9:00-10:00pm Mon-Fri

Food Deals 3
$3.00-$9.00
YAY! Another one of Portland's very best chefs started Happy Hour in a wonderful restaurant! Deliciously-spiced fried garbanzo beans, almonds, olives, or fried cauliflower; falafel, hummus, salads, lamb sandwich or lamb burger.

Drink Specials 3
$1.00 off drafts; $6.00 wines; $6.00 cocktails

Atmosphere 3
Dine at the bar or enjoy the seasonal patio. Overall, the space is beautiful and understated. Strong design using creative blends of woods, dark metals, glass and concrete. Warm and inviting, yet with a slightly cosmopolitan feel.

Why I really like it
Nice space and great food. Really great food!

Lincoln

North/NE Map
3808 N Williams, #127
(503) 288-6200
www.lincolnpdx.com

Happy Hours
5:30–7:00pm Tues–Fri

Food Deals 3
$3.00–$10.00
Americana home cooking with NW culinary bent and 20-item(!) seasonal, funky-fresh menu: baked eggs, pigs ears, fried chicken, poutine, carrot hummus, onion rings. Chef/owner Jenn Louis was named a Food & Wine Best New Chef in 2012, and has a new cookbook out, "Pasta by Hand".

Drink Specials 3
$4.00 microbrews; $5.00 house wines
$5.00 wells; $6.00 specialty cocktail

Atmosphere 3
Renovated loft-style warehouse space. Lincoln's interior is on the more basic side of industrial chic, but warmth is added via dark-red walls, natural woods, friendly staff and votive candles. Happy Hour in bar area (not restricted to bartop).

Why I really like it
I'm saying it again – *the food!* A giant array available at Happy Hour, and this is a good place to spring for dinner too.

SAT / ALL SUN

Mama Mia Trattoria

Downtown (East) Map
439 SW 2nd Ave.
(503) 295-6464
www.mamamiatrattoria.com

~ 2016 ~
TOP 10
Superstar

Happy Hours
4–7pm Mon–Sat; ★4:00–9:00pm Sun

GOLDEN TICKET!

Food Deals 3+ $2.25-$5.95
Astounding 20-item menu set up to nibble or enjoy an appetizer, salad, entree, *and* dessert – all at Happy Hour prices! Daily lasagna, linguine, manicotti, clams, mussels, minestrone, calamari, plus desserts including their trademark zeppole!

Drink Specials 3 $3.25-$4.50 drafts; $4.50 wine
$3.25 wells; $5.50-$6.50 cocktails (seven choices)

Atmosphere 3
Mama mia! Now that's Italian! Luscious old world ambiance with 20 chandeliers, golden touches, white marble tables, and romantic candlelight. Happy Hour is in the front bar area only, plus seasonal sidewalk al fresco dining. Group availability possible (must call ahead).

Why I really like it
You've probably heard all about it and tried it by now... they were Happy Hour of the Year 2015 for so many reasons! Great food, traditional Italian ambiance, and just kind of perfect in every way.

SAT-SUN

Manzana Grill

Lake Oswego
305 1st St.
(503) 675-3322
www.manzanagrill.com

GOLDEN TICKET!

Happy Hours
2:00–6:00pm and 9:00pm–close Daily

Food Deals 3
$1.95–$8.95
About 15 choices with substance and flavor make it hard to choose! Three kinds of street tacos, cheeseburgers, chorizo & peppers skillet, chili, tostadas, wings, fish & chips, calamari, ribs.

Drink Specials 3
$3.95 drafts; $4.95 red & white wine
$5.95 wells; $5.95 featured cocktails (4)

Atmosphere 3
Mmmm... the rotisserie smell! Deep, dark, rich wooden booths and walls (new and modern). Big space attracts a crowd. Located right on the lake and Happy Hour seating outside! Part of the esteemed Restaurants Unlimited Group.

Why I Really Like It
Such an array of good eats at low prices, with a lovely outdoor patio and peaceful lake view, all in a cozy and friendly space.

Marmo

Downtown (East)
1037 SW Morrison
(503) 224-0654
www.marmopdx.com

Happy Hours
3:00-6:30pm Tues-Sat

Food Deals 1
$1.00 off the whole menu of snacks, salads, sandwiches, small plate entrees, and sweets. Italian-cafe-driven food, and despite having cocktails, they close by 8:00pm. I like the concept of blanket discounting a whole menu, but needs to be more like 30% off to get me in early.

Drink Specials 2
$4.00 beer; $7.00 wine: $21 carafe

Atmosphere 3
Marmo means "marble" in Italian, and the place is full of the white shiny stuff, giving it a super-clean and fresh look. Pops of black and glass keep up the very modern coffee house effect.

New this Year/First Impressions
It seems targeted more for an after-and-during-work-oriented crowd with its daytime cafe feel.

Masu Sushi

SAT-SUN

Downtown (West) Map
406 SW 13th Ave.
(503) 221-6278
www.masusushi.com

Happy Hours
3:00–6:00pm Daily (4:00-6:00pm Sat-Sun)

Food Deals 3+
$3.00–$9.00
Possibly the best sushi in the city! Choose from about 30 options of nigiri and sushi maki rolls at Happy Hour. You will obviously want to choose several, and always consider sharing to enjoy even more.

Drink Specials 1
$4.50 Sapporo

Atmosphere 3
Unique retro-Asian lounge; open and boxy with Jenga-style wood blocks covering the walls and back bar; stunning, colorful, hand-painted mural. Ultra cool!

Why I really like it
My first time here, I walked in not liking sushi much, and walked out loving it! And now I always order too much when I go. Plus it's near Living Room Theaters which shows awesome movies :-)

McCormick & Schmick's
Harborside at the Marina

Willamette River
0309 SW Montgomery
(503) 220-1865
www.mccormickandschmicks.com

~ 2016 ~
TOP 10
Superstar

Happy Hours
3:00–6:00pm and 9:00–10:00pm Daily
(Until 11:00pm Fri-Sat)

Food Deals 3 $3.00-$9.00

Very extensive menu that changes occasionally, with items like bruschetta, fish or shrimp tacos, calamari, seared tuna, crab dip, wings, mussels, but then you almost always have to get their famous cheeseburger and fries for only $5 bucks!

Drink Specials 3
$4.00 Full Sail Amber draft (former brewery site)
$6.00 wine; $6.00–$7.00 cocktails

Atmosphere 3
Gorgeous and stately restaurant overlooking the Willamette River! Impressive, traditional-style. Happy Hour inside, on bar side. Classy, but fun. Worth a splurge on full dinner to dine outside.

Beaverton Location
9945 SW Beav-Hills Highway; (503) 643-1322

Tigard Location
17015 SW 72nd Ave.; (503) 684-5490
Suburb locations start Happy Hour at 4:00pm

McMenamin's Pubs

Select favorites – McMenamin's is a book in itself!
They all have HH but just go whenever. Not expensive.

Bagdad Theater/Greater Trumps
3702 SE Hawthorne; (503) 236-9234
Arabian-Nights-inspired movie theater and secret pub.

Blue Moon Tavern
432 NW 21st Ave.; (503) 223-3184
Meandering bar with table-top fireplace in the round and pool tables; outdoor sidewalk seating.

Chapel Pub
430 N Killingsworth; (503) 286-0372
A sanctuary with lots of cozy rooms. Outdoor patio.

Crystal Ballroom
1332 W Burnside; (503) 225-0047
Awesome place to see concerts! The ballroom floor is spring-loaded so it bounces slightly.

McMenamins on the Columbia
1801 SE Columbia River Dr.
Vancouver, WA; (360) 699-1521 Brews with views!

McMenamins Tavern & Pool
1716 NW 23rd Ave.; (503) 227-0929
Heated outdoor tables; big pool room.

Mission Theater
1624 NW Glisan; (503) 223-4527
$3.00 movies in old Swedish evangelical mission.

Ram's Head
2282 NW Hoyt; (503) 221-0098
Sophisticated manly-man haven.

Ringler's Pub (and Ringlers Annex across street)
1332 W. Burnside; (503) 225-0627
Funky ex-auto garage.

Zeus Café
303 SWt 12th Ave.; (503) 384-2500
The latest and greatest in the Crystal Hotel.

McMenamins Hotels

Crystal Hotel
303 SW 12th Ave.; Downtown Portland; (503) 972-2670
Right across the street from the Crystal Ballroom.
Houses Al's Den for live music and the Zeus Café too.

Edgefield
2126 SW Halsey; Troutdale; (503) 669-8610
38-acre renovated "Poor Farm;" golf course, movie
theater, beer garden, casual and fine-dining, wine bar,
Jerry Garcia bar, Little Red Shed Pub, and Spa.

Gearhart Hotel
1157 N. Marion Ave; Gearhart (coast); (503) 717-8150
Eighteen guestrooms on a golf course with pub.

Grand Lodge
3505 Pacific Ave.; Forest Grove; (503) 992-9533
Stately ex-Masonic lodge and nursing home near
Wine Country; restaurants, bars, movies, soak tub.

Hotel Oregon
310 NE Evans Street; McMinnville; (503) 472-8427
Weekend get-away in wine country; rooftop bar (great
for viewing UFOs), pub, back bar, Cellar Bar, billiards.

Kennedy School
5736 NE 33rd Ave.; Portland; (503) 249-3983
Detention Bar, Honors Bar, Boiler Room Bar, movies,
soaking pool, beer garden, party rooms, restaurant.

Old St. Francis School
700 NW Bond; Bend; (541) 382-5174
Old 1936 Catholic schoolhouse transformed into
a heavenly entertainment complex.

White Eagle
836 N. Russell; Portland (503) 335-8900
A small "rock 'n' roll hotel" with resident "spirits"
(it's reportedly haunted), nightly bands, saloon,
and outdoor, seasonal beer garden.

SAT-SUN

Meriwether's

NW/Nob Hill Map
2601 NW Vaughn
(503) 228-1250
www.meriwethersnw.com

Happy Hours
4:00-6:00pm Daily

Food Deals 3+
$3.00–$12.00
OMGWOW! 16 "Pantry Board" items to mix and mingle and another 12 appetizers and such! Seasonal deliciousness like soup, olives, deviled eggs, several salads, fries, burger, stuffed dates, pizza, ribs, steak bites, foccacia, fried pickles, fritters, polenta fries, walnut dip, falafel and more!

Drink Specials 2
$1.00 off drafts; $5.00 select wine

Atmosphere 3
Built on the site of the 1905 World's Fair. Their historic and stately interior exudes a warm and hospitable countryside inn quality. Impressive! Incredibly cozy in the winter. Gorgeous deck out back, but not available for Happy Hour.

Why I really like it
I love the insane variety you can get here, all served in cute little terrine bowls on a big wooden pantry board.

Mother's

Downtown (East) Map
212 SW Stark
(503) 464-1122
www.mothersbistro.com

Happy Hours
3:00–7:00pm Tues–Fri

Food Deals 3
$3.50
Fried ravioli, chicken quesadilla, mini-burgers, deviled eggs, hummus, fries, chopped liver, pulled pork sliders, and little teenie weenies :-)

Drink Specials 3
$4.00 microbrew pints; $6.00 wines
$5.00 array of infused cocktails

Atmosphere 3
Their "Velvet Lounge" bar side steps back in time and looks much like a wealthy, Southern grandmother's home. High ceilings, brick walls, ornate gilded mirrors, chandeliers, and flocked wallpaper everywhere. Cool space!

Why I really like it
It's a classic, tried-and-true Happy Hour in the lounge side of wonderful Mother's Restaurant. It's all about the love!

Muselet/Soirée

South Waterfront (of map)
3730 SW Bond Ave.
(503) 265-8133
www.museletpdx.com

Happy Hours
4:00-6:00pm Tues-Sat

Food Deals 3
$1.50-$8.00
The full line-up of all trending cocktail bar food. About a dozen samplings including pork belly, hen rillette, pork terrine, oysters, warm olives, chicken liver mousse, steak bites, cheese plate.

Drink Specials 3
$6.00 wines; $20 bottles; $6.00 select cocktail

Atmosphere 3
Stunning and gorgeous! You get the feeling you are not in Portland anymore in this metropolitan-swanky Soirée lounge, in the back of one of our city's most heralded new restaurants, Muselet. Lots of black, with a fascinating chandelier of about 100 wine bottle lights.

New this Year/First Impressions
I'm impressed they are even offering a Happy Hour, as their dinner here is so complex and innovative. I love the look here – totally cosmopolitan, cool, contemporary, classy. The perfect backdrop for wine or martini sipping.

SAT-SUN

Nel Centro

Downtown (West) Map
1408 SW 6th Avenue
(503) 484-1099
www.nelcentro.com

Happy Hours
4:00–6:00pm Daily

Food Deals 3
$3.00–$7.00
Seasonal 15-item menu from one of Portland's most respected kitchens: delicious gourmet-style pizzas (choice of four), lamb burger, meatballs, mussels, soup, pork slider, calamari, and salads.

Drink Specials 3
$4.00 drafts; $6.00 house wines and prosecco
$5.00 featured cocktail or well drinks

Atmosphere 3
One of the most enjoyable patios in town where you can enjoy Happy Hour too! Next to the Hotel Modera with mod, contemporary courtyard and long fire pits. Inside, the decor is sleek and stylish, with a giant open bar and globe lights.

Why I really like it
Inside and out, impressive and well-designed. Across the board, it never fails as an enjoyable and tasty place to go for Happy Hour.

SAT-SUN

Night Light Lounge

Southeast Map
2100 SE Clinton
(503) 731-6500
www.nightlightlounge.net

Happy Hours
★2:00–7:00pm Daily (3:00-7:00pm Sat–Sun)
11:00pm–1:00am Sun–Thurs

Food Deals 2
$3.00–$5.00
Soup, salad, grilled cheese, Caesar salad, quesadilla, mac & cheese, nachos.

Drink Specials 2
$4.00 microbrews; $1.50 PBRs;
$.50 off well drinks; $1.00 off wine

Atmosphere 2
Simple, artsy, casual, comfortable, yet trendy. All-season outdoor dining on heated back deck! Or enjoy the open air in the summer when the tent top is unveiled for sunshine.

Why I really like it
Quality ingredients, good taste, and low prices! It's casual for my usual preferences, but in a good way. Pleasant.

Noble Rot

Lloyd Center-ish Map
1111 E Burnside
(503) 233-1999
www.noblerotpdx.com

Happy Hours
5:00–6:00pm Mon–Fri

Food Deals 3
$2.00–$10.00
Expanded menu ranges from nibblets to comfort food adapts for each season: onion rings, French fries, fish cakes, salads, pickle plate, exceptional paninos, mac & cheese, hamburger.

Drink Specials 3
$4.00 draft beer; $4.00 red or white wine
$5.50 selection of bartender's specialties

Atmosphere 3
Stunning wall-to-wall, floor-to-ceiling windows perched high for a wide-open city view; ultra-cool contemporary-retro interior; illuminated circular glass art on ceiling. Rooftop outdoor deck with Happy Hour seating (and working garden)! Sunset Magazine's Best Wine Bar 2009.

Why I really like it
See above – what's not to love?!

Noho's Hawaiian Cafe

SAT-SUN

Fremont Map
4627 NE Fremont
(503) 445-6646
www.nohos.com

Happy Hours
3:00-6:00pm Daily (opens 4:00pm Mon)

Food Deals 2
$3.95 Pork or chicken spring rolls or sliders
$4.95 Ribs or grilled chicken
$7.95 Hawaiian style or shoyu poke, sashimi plate

Drink Specials 3
$4.00 drafts; $5.00 wine; $7.00 mai tais

Atmosphere 3+
Awesome back patio area! Head out back whenever possible. The interior has surfboards hanging on the walls, and is on the more casual side. Heads up -- there are two Portland locations, but this is the one I love! Plus, it's a *really* great place to have a party!!!

Why I really like it
One of Portland's best-kept secrets! Out back, there's a surprise, very lush, tropical garden complete with palm trees, hanging lights, and a group firepit. Seriously -- you'll feel like you've stepped into a Hawaiian vacation! Heated in the winter, but nicest in the summer.

SAT-SUN / ALL MON

North 45

~ 2016 ~
TOP 10
Superstar

NW/Nob Hill Map
517 NW 21st Ave.
(503) 248-6317
www.north45pub.com

Happy Hours
4:00–6:00pm Daily; ★All night Mon

Food Deals 3
$4.00–$7.00
Ten tasty treats from all over the globe! They'll change here and there, but you'll enjoy things like flautas, calamari, green beans, ceviche, wings, mac & cheese, dips, and fresh salads.

Drink Specials 3
$4.00 pints of Trumer Pilsner; $5.00 house wines $4.00 wells; $6.00 "Patio-Rita"

Atmosphere 3
A rich, but homey feel to their travelers-themed bar with framed maps and vacation photos. Very cozy inside/huge patio beer garden in back – which is tented and heated in the winter.

Why I Really Like It
Lots of Belgian beers! And I always want to plan a long trip when I'm here and see all the pictures from places fellow patrons have visited, as pinned all over the map and bulletin boards. Plus I'm loving the Thursday guest breweries sampling free tastes out back (through Spring).

SAT-SUN / ALL TUES

North Light

North/NE Map
3746 N Mississippi
(503) 477-7079
www.northlightpdx.com

Happy Hours
4:00-7:00pm Tues-Sun; ★4:00pm-close Tues

Food Deals 3
$2.00-$9.00
Nice line up of delicious garlic fries, two salad choices, corn fritters, crispy chicken lollipops (gluten-free too!), mac & cheese, cheeseburger.

Drink Specials 2
$1.00 off beer, wine, and wells

Atmosphere 3
From the owners of the beloved Night Light in SE. Contemporary, fresh spin on somewhat seventies style, with vinyl booth seating, giant drum lights overhead, and little orange glass candle lights flickering and floating on a big white wall. Perfectly wonderful outdoor patio that includes a super-long bartop which is great for groups.

Why I Really Like It
I like the streamlined, clean style of the interior. And I *love* the patio! Plus... they have Bloody Marys for only $2.00 at weekend brunch!

Nostrana

Southeast Map
1401 SE Morrison
(503) 234-2427
www.nostrana.com

Happy Hours 9:00pm–close Daily (Nightly)

Food Deals 3
$3.00–$9.00
Late-night-only Happy Hour from Cathy Whims, SIX-time James Beard Award Finalist! She also owns Oven & Shaker, and it's all about the wood-fired pizza here too. Get the chef's special, marinara, or margherita style (optional add-ons include add arugula, prosciutto, olives). Also: salad, pastas, nuts, roasted olives and cheeses.

Drink Specials 3
$5.00 seasonal ale or pils; $5.00 house wines
$3.00 fresh lemonade; $5.00 select cocktails

Atmosphere 3
Giant, hanger-like space in a mini strip mall with an overhead, complex grid of wood ceiling beams. Interior still manages to feel friendly and intimate with candles, suspended framed art, and a long, communal bar with giant, towering shelves.

Why I Really Like It
It's so good, and so enjoyable. It's so late, but it adds to the ambiance (and appetite)!

SAT / ALL SUN

Oba!

A PERFECT 10
10 YEARS
– and counting –

Pearl Map
555 NW 12th Ave.
(503) 228-6161
www.obarestaurant.com

Happy Hours
4:00–6:30pm Daily; 4:00pm–close Sundays ★
9:00pm–close Mon–Thurs; 10pm-close Fri-Sat

Food Deals 3
$4.00–$6.00
A forever classic! Giant menu of deliciousness (careful – you'll easily leave too full): Oba Caesar, grilled sweet corn, chicken or fish tacos, corn cakes with pork & cabbage, nachos, and more.

Drink Specials 3
$5.00 drafts; $6.00 house wine
$5.00 flavored Margaritas or mojitos

Atmosphere 3
Colorful, Latin-American-style with a festive and trendy scene. Golden and terra cotta walls, pillars and white sparkly tree lights. Outdoor sidewalk dining. "The kind of place you need to hit before confession."

Why I Really Like It
It's the second-ever Happy Hour I hit when I first moved to Portland, and it continues to be a high standard I compare other places to. Mostly I love all the exciting *flavor!*

Oven & Shaker

Pearl Map
1134 NW Everett
(503) 241-1600
www.ovenandshaker.com

Happy Hours
2:30-5:30pm Mon-Fri; 10:00pm–close Daily

Food Deals 3
$7.00–$10.00
Phenomenally delicious wood-fired pizza, as brought to us by Cathy Whims of Nostrana (Four-time James Beard nominee). About half-off several pizza styles with unique, gourmet spins. A couple of fresh and healthy salads too.

Drink Specials 3
$3.00 daily draft; $5.00 wine; $7.00 cocktails

Atmosphere 3
Rough, exposed woods cover the place with rustic urban charm. An ultra-long bar (45-feet) dominates one full wall, with windows open to the street along the front. Enormously popular and delicious, it's nice they offer a break.

Why I Really Like It
Good deals on interesting pizza with salads too. Personally, I prefer it next door at Piattino, but this place gets so many rave reviews you'll need to do your own tests time and time again.

SAT-SUN

Paadee

Lloyd Center-ish Map
6 SE 28th Ave.
(503) 360-1453
www.paadeepdx.com

Happy Hours
5:00–6:00pm Daily

Food Deals 3
$2.00–$7.00
Excellent choices and well-made: Grilled squid or pork skewers, tom yum soup, sausage selections, fish cakes, noodle dishes. Award-winning food at a top PDX restaurant!

Drink Specials 3
$4.00 drafts; $5.00 house wines
$6.00 specialty cocktails

Atmosphere 3
Cozy industrial-chic, with talented and appropriate interior design choices incorporating subtle Asian stylings. Lots of light, cool bar, curtains, flowers, stained concrete. Long wood tables for groups, smaller 2-4 tops, and sidewalk seating.

Why I Really Like It
Really-really-really great Thai food! All that, and it's further escalated up to new heights at their restaurant next door, Langbaan (no Happy Hour there though).

Paddy's Bar & Grill

SAT-SUN

Downtown (East) Map
65 SW Yamhill
(503) 224-5626
www.paddys.com

Happy Hours
4:00–6:30pm Daily

Food Deals 3
$3.00–$7.00
Greatly expanded Happy Hour menu, including six kinds of flavored mac & cheese! Also tots, Irish empanadas, shepherd's pie, reuben sliders or dip, poppers, poutine, mini-burgers, nachos, calamari.

Drink Specials 2
$4.00 pils; $6.00 wine; $6.50 Irish Mule

Atmosphere 3
Warm, upscale Irish pub with a very impressive turn-of-the-century bar stacked sky-high with spirits of all sorts. Seasonal sidewalk seating.

Why I Really Like It
I'm half-Irish, and Paddy's has a nice, old-world feel to it. It's a big rainy day go-to. On Mondays, there's traditional Irish music sessions starting at 7:00pm!

SAT-SUN

Paley's Place

Pearl Map
1204 NW 21st Ave.
(503) 243-2403
www.paleysplace.net

Happy Hours
5:30-6:30pm Mon-Thur; 5:00-6:30pm Fri-Sun

Food Deals 3
$2.00-$7.00
Wow! One of the city's best chefs and most lovely places offers Happy Hour in the bar! Owned by Vitaly Paley, a James Beard award-winner, offers a most excellent cheeseburger, oysters on the half shell, fries, seasonal salads and veggies, bruschetta, cheeses. Ask to see the dinner menu – it's surprisingly affordable!

Drink Specials 3
$3.00 select beers; $5.00 wine: $6.00 cocktails

Atmosphere 3
Opened in 1995 in a large, traditional-style home with large wrap-around porch. He has a good cookbook to try: "The Paley's Place Cookbook: Recipes and Stories from the Pacific Northwest".

Why I Really Like It
It's quiet and mellow and refined. And it's Paley.

Pambiche

Lloyd Center-ish Map
2811 NE Glisan
(503) 233-0511
www.pambiche.com

Happy Hours
★2:00–6:00pm Mon–Fri; 10:00pm–mid Fri–Sat

Food Deals 3+
$2.00–$5.00
Exceptionally delicious menu of 17 items: Mmmmpenadas, fried plantains, salads, bean and rice dishes, fried chicken and pork, shredded beef, stew—and don't miss the desserts!

Drink Specials 3
$2.50 Tecate; $5.00 wine; $6.00 sangrias
$5.50-$7.00 select cocktails
$1.00 off espressos, teas, sodas, juices & shakes

Atmosphere 3
Fun and colorful Cuban café! Outdoor dining area streetside; bright, cozy and happy inside; vibrant exterior. Captures the Cuban "feel" well.

Why I Really Like It
The FLAVOR and lots of it! Unique menu items not served elsewhere.

Papa Haydn

NW/Nob Hill Map
701 NW 23rd Ave.; (503) 228-7317

<u>Sellwood</u> 5829 SE Milwaukee; (503) 232-9440
(Similar menu 3:00–6:00pm Daily)
www.papahaydn.com

Happy Hours
3:00–6:00pm Mon–Fri

Food Deals 3
$2.00–$7.00
A Portland favorite since 1983 with a most excellent, high-quality Happy Hour! Good size menu with French onion soup, salad, burger, clams, fries, croque monseur or madam (with turkey), mushroom bolognese.

Drink Specials 3
$4.00 drafts; $6.50 wines and wells
$5.00–$6.00 house cocktails

Atmosphere 3
Everything cute in traditional design is represented and ties together beautifully: buttercream walls, upholstered seats, paned glass, thick mouldings, stripes and harlequin patterns, and carpeting.

Why I Really Like It
It's a very sweet and serene spot, and well-known reputation for delicious desserts!

Park Kitchen

Old Town
422 NW 8th Ave
(503) 223-7275
www.parkkitchen.com

Happy Hours
5:00–6:00pm Daily

Food Deals 3
$4.00-8.00
Small, changing menu with just a few seasonal, Americana-nouveau small plates like fried green beans with bacon and tarragon aioli, flank steak salad, soups, terrine, or salt cod fritters. Bring a friend and get one of everything!

Drink Specials 2
$6.00 wine; $6.00 cocktails

Atmosphere 3
Cute, candlelit, and cozy! Coming in from the streets, it's such a sweet, subdued, almost-country respite inside. Café tables outside, with garage doors that open to the park blocks.

Why I Really Like It
Off the beaten path, but not by much. One of Portland's best restaurants. Two-time James Beard nominee.

Peddler & The Pen

Downtown (East)
2327 NW Kearney
(503) 477-4380
www.thepeddlerandpen.com

Happy Hours
3:00-6:00pm and 10:00pm-close Daily

Food Deals 2
$4.00 Any Appetizer
Currently six choices of old writer pub faves: Poe's pickles, Tennyson's toast, Kerouac's kebabs, Scotch eggs, pub chips, curry fries.

Drink Specials 2
$3.00 High Life (um...why?); $4.00 Moscow Mule
$4.00 wine; $4.00 wells

Atmosphere 2
Formerly Laurelwood NW and Huckleberry Tavern. Cute place in an old home, but bar service makes the ambiance awkward. Could be a cozy, quiet, writerly place on a rainy day; or in the heat of July, enjoy the patio or upper deck's balcony.

New this Year/First Impressions
I love this little house, but it's not fixed up to its true potential in this new rendition. And the food is just so-so with odd choices. So far...

Petisco

North/NE Map
1411 NE Broadway
(503) 360-1048
www.petiscopdx.com

Happy Hours
3:00–6:00pm Tues–Sat

Food Deals 3+
$6.00
Ten superb sandwiches served hot or cold, choice of bread, and can be requested as, or with, salads. Two exceptional prosciutto options, roasted portobello, roast beef with roasted red peppers, ham and brie, or deluxe chicken salad. So good! I can never go long without going here.

Drink Specials 2
$2.00 Millers; $5.00 house wines; $4.00 sangrias

Atmosphere 2
Cute and casual with European ambiance. Half-sunken basement gives the place added coziness, with a fun patio down below street level. Exposed brick walls, open kitchen and chalkboard menus.

Why I Really Like It
Such a deal on such delicious sandwiches! Served with side salads no less, and SO good! Good dinners. And brunches. Lunches too :-)

Piattino

Pearl Map
1140 NW Everett
(971) 983-8000
www.piattinopdx.com

Happy Hours
3:00–5:30pm Tues-Sat

Food Deals 3
$4.00–$12.00
Italian small-plates restaurant offers big plate deals on five of their famously fabulous wood-fired thin crust pizzas, plus mussels, antipasti boards, salads, crostini, gnocchi, fettucini, and bread (made fresh in-house, like their pasta).

Drink Specials 2
$5.00 beer; $6.00-$7.00 wine; $7.00 cocktails

Atmosphere 3
Warm and woody space with gorgeous wood tables, reclaimed wood fully covering the walls, and a wood-fired pizza oven front and center. You can see the kitchen and watch them cook from the 11th St. window. Interesting to watch.

Why I Really Like It
Quality ingredients served with pride and love. Nice owner and staff.

Pine Shed Ribs

Downtown (East)
17730 Pilkington Rd.
(503) 635-7427
www.pineshedribs.com

Happy Hours
4:00-7:00pm Mon-Sat

Food Deals 3
$2.50-$6.00
Limited menu, but perfect size to go with a friend and get one of each! Jumbo chicken wings, gorgonzola smoked bacon wedge, BBQ ribs, and loaded pork sliders (the best in town)! Be sure to get some of their incredible cornbread too!

Drink Specials 3
$1.00 off bottles and drafts; $2.00 cans
$7.00 microbrew sampler; $5.00 wine

Atmosphere 2
Roadhouse style, but oddly set in a strip mall. A working smoking shed to the side with fun patio seating. Restaurant entrance is two doors down from shed. Inside is homey and welcoming, with standard NW decor of reclaimed woods and a cement floor, plus some cute southern kitchen kitsch. Not brand-new, but new to book.

New this Year/First Impressions
I'm going to get cravings whenever I'm nearby! Dry rub, authentic flavor, 12-hour slow roasted.

ALL TUES

Pink Rose

Pearl Map
1300 NW Lovejoy
(503) 482-2165
www.facebook.com/pinkrosepearl

Happy Hours
4:00-7:00pm Mon-Fri / 10:00pm–mid Tues-Sat
★All night Tuesday

Food Deals 3
$3.00-$10.00
Too many popular house favorites to change the menu much: pork fries, salads, grilled Brussels sprouts, stuffed shrooms, bacon-wrapped dates, burgers, fries, cheese plate.

Drink Specials 2
$4.00 drafts; $5.00 wines; $5.00 wells

Atmosphere 3
A few years ago, this was the ultra-hip SoLo. It's lost some edge and is softer now, but still retains an underground, clubby look and feel. The upstairs deck is lovely in the summer, with its pink umbrella tables, torches, heat lamps, potted plants and the elevated view of Lovejoy action.

Why I Really Like It
Simple and simply works. And somehow always right in my path! Just need more sunny days...

SAT / ALL SUN

Portland City Grill

Downtown (East) Map
111 SW Fifth Ave., 30th Floor
(503) 450-0030
www.portlandcitygrill.com

Happy Hours
4:00–7:00pm and 9:00pm–close Mon–Sat
★Noon–11:00pm Sunday

Food Deals 3
$4.95–$9.95
About 15 high-quality and beautifully-presented apps like salmon cakes, spring rolls, fries, cheeseburger, spicy garlic chicken w/noodles, fish & chips, riblets, steak sandwich, kung pao calamari, sushi roll, ahi tuna, salads, and dessert.

Drink Specials 3
$5.25 draft; $6.95 wines; $5.95 special cocktails

Atmosphere 3+
Get there early and try to get a window seat! Enjoy amazing views of our city, river, hills, Mt. Hood, sunsets, and occasional full moons. Giant central bar, full walls of windows, raw timber beams, marble cocktail tables, and live piano music.

Why I Really Like It
Impressive! Not fair to compare. They blow the curve for everyone else. Their prices have crept up a bit, but still doesn't keep the large crowds down. Continual note to self – all day Sunday!

Portland Penny Diner

New!

Downtown (East) Map
410 SW Broadway
(503) 228-7224
www.imperialpdx.com/portland-penny-diner

Happy Hours
4:00–6:00pm Mon-Sat

Food Deals 3
$5.00-$6.00
An ever changing menu will offer a soup or salad, and several fry bread sandwiches: pork belly (won the 2015 People's Choice Award at Feast), chicken shawarma, black bean, fried oysters.

Drink Specials 3
$5.00 drafts; $7.00 wine; $5.00-$6.00 cocktails

Atmosphere 3
Shiny diner style done with big city coolness. From Vitaly Paley (one of Portland's best chefs that also owns Imperial right next door). Named after the infamous coin flip between 1845 city founders Pettygrove and Lovejoy. We could have been called Boston instead!

New Happy Hour this Year/First Impressions
After three years, they expanded their breakfast and lunch menu to include Happy Hour, dinner, and reputable craft cocktails. The fry bread sandwiches are to die for!

Portland Prime

Downtown (East) Map
121 SW 3rd Ave.
(503) 223-6200
www.portlandprime.net

GOLDEN TICKET!

Happy Hours
3:00–7:00pm Mon-Fri; 1:00-6:00pm Sun

Food Deals 3
$3.00-$8.00
Prime bar menu offers a wide array of tasty bar apps and meals: burgers, wings, Cajun fettucine, hush puppies, stuffed potato skins, poppers, hummus, Caesar, steak quesadilla, onion rings.

Drink Specials 3
$5.00 drafts; $6.00 house wines
$7.00 wells; $7.00 signature cocktails

Atmosphere 3
Located in Embassy Suites – enter through the lobby as it's majestic! Rich mahogany woods and private booth seating; enjoy elegant restaurant dining on the cheap! Several hi-def TVs.

Why I Really Like It
Old-school steak house style. Dark and mellow, comfortable but classy.

Pour Wine Bar

Lloyd Center-ish Map
2755 NE Broadway
(503) 288-7687
www.pourwinebar.com

Happy Hours
4:30–6:00pm Tues–Sat

Food Deals 2
$3.00
Big bowls of little nibbles like marinated olives, Inca corn, and roasted hazelnuts. Regular menu has delicious and affordable dinner options, and should really just be called a Happy Hour menu.

Drink Specials 3
$4.00 wine; $3.00 select beer

Atmosphere 3
Striking and sleek 1960s-style Space Odyssey lounge; mod design with cool, white retro chairs and walls; string art mural; silver, candlelight, and real flowers.

Why I Really Like It
The owner Robert knows and loves his wine – and loves to share his knowledge and fantastic finds! It's all about the wine here, and you'll be very impressed by your $4.00 pour! Be sure to try his Thursday night wine tastings!

Produce Row Café

Central Eastside
204 SE Oak St.
(503) 232-8355
www.producerowcafe.com

Happy Hours
4:00-7:00pm and 10:00pm–close (food) Daily
★All night Monday

GOLDEN TICKET!

Food Deals 3
$4.00–$6.00
Tavern menu with food that goes all too well with beer: beer batter fries, BBQ wings, tots, salad, beer cheese mac, nachos, chili.

Drink Specials 3
$4.00 select beer; $5.00 wine
$6.00-$8.00 cocktails (5)

Atmosphere 3
Turn-of-the-century beer hall charm mixed with urban Portland vibe. Gorgeous, mahogany front bar with beer selections written on giant mirror. Tin ceilings, with wooden beams, tables and floors. The back patio is a top favorite of many!

New Happy Hour this Year/First Impressions
New management brings a whole new life to this Portland landmark cafe (owners from North 45, The Station, Circa 33, Paddy's). It has fully shed its dive bar dust and now shines once more. Extensive whiskey and beer pairing menu!

SAT / ALL SUN

Ringside Glendoveer

Glendoveer
14021 NE Glisan
(503) 255-0750
www.ringsidesteakhouse.com

Happy Hours
3:00–6:00 pm and 8:30pm–close Daily
★11:30am-6:30pm Sat; 11:30am-close Sun★

Food Deals 3+
$2.25-4.95
16 menu items: steak bites (YUM!), calamari, burger, potato skins, soup, quesadilla, baked brie, prime rib dip, crab cake, cheeseburger, steamed clam strips, oysters, shrimp, and more!

Drink Specials 3
$5.00 drafts; $6.00 red or white wine,
select well drinks, margaritas or Manhattan

Atmosphere 3
Less dramatic, but bigger and more open than downtown location with dark, wood paneling and wall-to-wall windows. Big, open fireplace. Views of on-site golf course. Great enclosed patio with wonderful outdoor seating all around!

Why I Really Like It
It's next to the Glendoveer Golf Course and Driving Range so makes for a fun combo, especially with the daytime weekend Happy Hours!

Ringside Fish House

NW/Nob Hill Map
838 SW Park Ave. (Fox Tower)
(503) 227-3900
www.ringsidefishhouse.com

Happy Hours
3:00pm–6:30pm and 9:00pm-close Daily
★3:00pm–close Sunday

Food Deals 3+
$2.95–$4.95
Big menu of 12 or so items: steak bites (YUM!), steamed mussels, shrimp, fried oysters, Caesar salad, burger, fish tacos, clam chowder, salmon slider, deviled eggs, calamari, or French dip

Drink Specials 3
$1.00 off drafts; $6.00 wine or wells

Atmosphere 3
Contemporary, upscale, toned-down interior with Happy Hour in bar area only. Illuminated, colorful ceramic fish and giant whale bone decorate the walls. A Happy Hour must!

Why I Really Like It
Surely, you must know it, so just a reminder with this one! The NW Ringside Steak House is great too, but HH is after 9:30pm except on Sundays (4:00-5:30pm).

SAT-SUN / ALL TUES

Riverview

Sandy River / Troutdale
29311 SE Stark
(503) 661-FOOD (3663)
www.yoshidariverview.com

Happy Hours
4:00–7:00pm Tues-Sun; All night Tuesday ★

Food Deals 3
$3.00–$8.00
Nice mix of bar menu faves done gourmet-style and switched out seasonally: steak bites, salads, chowder, sliders, calamari, wontons, skewers.

Drink Specials 3
$4.50 beer; $5.00 wine; $5.00 select cocktails

Atmosphere 3+
An absolutely gorgeous place! Fine dining with views of the Sandy River and surrounding forest. The Happy Hour area is in the lounge side, and get there early to stake a seat outside on their lovely seasonal patio! Keep it in mind after a Sunday Gorge hike (unless your shoes are muddy 'cause it's fancy here)! Frequent live music.

Why I Really Like It
It's so beautiful! And such a deal too!

SAT/SUN

Ruth's Chris

Downtown (East) Map
850 SW Broadway
(503) 221-4518
www.ruthschris.com

~ 2016 ~
TOP 10
Superstar

Happy Hours
4:00–7:00pm Daily

Food Deals 3
$8.00
Six high-quality apps like seared ahi tuna, prime burger, tenderloin skewer salad, crab BLT, steak sandwich, or spicy lobster.

Drink Specials 3
$4.00 domestics; $8.00 red or white wine
$8.00 select cocktails

Atmosphere 3
This new and upgraded location gives us a wonderful and bright, richly-appointed, fine-dining steakhouse. Enjoy a very affordable, fancy evening out when you go here for their Happy Hour. Big cheers to the good life!

Why I Really Like It
Years ago, the manager at the old-school, dark-wood Ruth's Chris downtown location somehow got their first Happy Hour pushed through for approval. Now years later, most of their locations have a spectacular one, including this Top 10 favorite!

Saké

Downtown (West) Map
615 SW Park Ave; (503) 222-1391
SE Hawthorne Map
3272 SE Hawthorne; (503) 239-3909
www.sakethaior.com

Happy Hours
5:00–6:00pm Tues-Fri

Food Deals 3+ $2.00-$5.00
A most exceptionally delicious mix of Japanese and Thai cuisine! Includes spring rolls, salad, edamame, gyoza, crab rangoon, tom yum, tom kha, pad thai, fried rice, bok choy; plus tuna, veggie, salmon, or shrimp sushi rolls.

Drink Specials 3
$4.00 beer; $5.00 wine; $6.00 cocktails

Atmosphere 2
Downtown – It's is not incredibly polished on the outside, but a hidden gem on the inside! Simple and serene with gold walls and a big front bar. NEW! Hawthorne – Sake Izakaya is even more basic than downtown with one open room.

Why I Really Like It
The food here is truly delicious – high quality, very flavorful and well-made, and such an exciting wide variety at Happy Hour! You can get both Japanese and Thai at the same time, and it is *so* good!

Salty's

SAT-SUN

Columbia River
3839 NE Marine Drive
(503) 288-4444
www.saltys.com/portland

A PERFECT 10
10 YEARS
– and counting –

Happy Hours
3:00–6:00pm Mon–Fri; 8:00-close Fri (Mel Brown live jazz); 4:00-6:00 Sat; 4:30pm-6:00 Sun

Food Deals 3 $2.00–$9.00
More than a dozen superb menu items including a cup of award-winning seafood chowder (yum!), blackened salmon Caesar, fish & chips, fish taco, calamari, oysters, coconut prawns, fish tacos, daily flatbread, salad, and bacon cheeseburgers.

Drink Specials 3
$2.50 Session beer; $5.00 wine selections
$5.50 Select boat drinks

Atmosphere 3+
Fine-dining waterside restaurant; wall-to-wall giant windows and stellar outdoor deck; yacht club motif. Gorgeous scenery along the river, and a great place to watch the sunset!

Why I Really Like It
Happy Hour of the Year 2012! I literally bought my house (and my Happy Mermaid Gift Shop) in this area because it is so lovely here on the Columbia River. Check calendar for live music!

SAT-SUN

Salvador Molly's

Portland/Hillsdale (NW of Multnomah Village)
1523 SW Sunset Blvd.
(503) 293-1790
www.salvadormollys.com

Happy Hours
3:00–6:00pm and last hour Daily

Food Deals 3
$2.95-$4.95
YUM!! Unique nibbles from around the globe with all kinds of different and bold flavors! Revolving menu changes seasonally with about 6 items like rasta rings, nachos, salad, spicy tacos. Or this is new: Crisp garlic potato wedges topped with slow-cooked Tamarindo BBQ pork, cheese & sour cream (Won a Travel Channel competition!)

Drink Specials 2
$1.00 off drafts; $5.00 cocktail of the day

Atmosphere 3
International fun and flair! Bold vibrant colors in both food and decor. Entire walls and table tops are covered in worldly memorabilia. Happy Hour in bar side only or outside on the deck.

Why I Really Like It
The flavors! And that vacation-y feeling that's hard to come by simply by visiting a restaurant.

SAT-SUN

Sapphire Hotel

Southeast Map
5008 SE Hawthorne
(503) 232-6333
www.thesapphirehotel.com

Happy Hours
4:00–6:00pm Daily
10:00pm-close Sun–Thurs

Food Deals 3
$2.00–$6.00
Meze platters, soup, several salads, artichoke dip, five spice chicken, salmon corncakes.

Drink Specials 3
$5.00 drafts; $5.00 selected wine
$4.00 well drinks; $5.00-$6.00 cocktail specials

Atmosphere 3
Mysteriously sexy and intriguing; trés swanky! Intimate creative lounge decor. Ex-brothel. Outdoor sidewalk seating.

Why I Really Like It
The epitome of a cocktail lounge and it speaks to my gypsy artist soul :-) The best and most appropriate names of drinks in all the land!

Saucebox

Downtown (East) Map
214 SW Broadway
(503) 241-3393
www.saucebox.com

Happy Hours
4:30-6:30pm Tues-Fri; 5:00-6:30pm Sat

Food Deals 3+
$2.00–$6.00
A better-than-ever menu of about 20 mostly Asian-inspired fusion dishes: Salad, spring, or hand rolls, crispy Brussels sprouts, miso soup, taro chips, three sytles of pad thai, pork noodle, veggie curry, nigiri, and the best burgers!

Drink Specials 3
$3.00 select beer; $5.00 wine; $5.00 saké
$5.00 daily cocktail; $5.00 boxcar or daiquiri

Atmosphere 3
Big and open, boxy, saucy lounge; chocolate-browns and greys; looming giant art murals with personality overlook the entire room. Upstairs and sidewalk dining, too. Cool bathroom entrance!

Why I Really Like It
Once again, another perfect Happy Hour, from gifted owner Bruce Carey (23 Hoyt, Bluehour, Clarklewis). It's a classic, and *always* impresses.

SAT-SUN / ALL TUES

Seres

Pearl Map
1105 NW Lovejoy
(971) 222-7327
www.seresrestaurant.com

~ 2016 ~
TOP 10
Superstar

GOLDEN TICKET!

Happy Hours
3:00–7:00pm Mon–Sat
★All night Tues; 4:00-7:00pm Sun

Food Deals 3+
$2.00–$6.50
More than 20 cravable, high-quality, fresh and organic Pan Asian delights brings everything under the sun: salt & pepper pork, General Tso's chicken, Cantonese crispy prawns, spring or salad rolls, wonton soup, lo mein, pot stickers, string beans, soups, kung pao chicken, fried rice.

Drink Specials 3
$3.50 drafts; $6.00 wines; $7.00 select cocktails

Atmosphere 3
Pearlesque loft-style with Far East reserve. High-end but friendly and comfortable. Lofty loft space with full, floor-to-ceiling windows; natural tones and tables; gorgeous hanging tile art pieces.

Why I Really Like It
It's healthy and high-quality Chinese food, up a few tiers and on a whole different level than most Chinese restaurants!

SAT-SUN

Serratto

NW/Nob Hill Map
2112 NW Kearney
(503) 221-1195
www.serratto.com

Happy Hours
4:00–6:00pm Daily

Food Deals 3
$1.00–$10.00
More than a dozen positively stellar menu items: stone oven pizzas (2), flame-broiled burger, salad, calamari, hummus, stuffed peppers, French onion soup, spaghetti bolognese, shrimp, pommes frites, almonds, artisan bread w/oil.

Drink Specials 2
$5.00 red or white house wine; $5.00 wells
$5.00 simple cocktails (3)

Atmosphere 3
Happy Hour is in their more casual "Vineria" which is only slightly Italian in ambiance, but extremely pleasant and even romantic.

Why I Really Like It
It's so good! One that most people know about, but one that we all need to revisit.

Slide Inn

Lloyd Center-ish Map
2348 SE Ankeny
(503) 236-4997
www.slideinnpdx.com

Happy Hours
5:30–6:30pm Daily; ★All night Mon-Tues

Food Deals 3 $4.00–$8.00
Extensive menu with gluten-free and veggie options. Also, some heavy aprés ski food. Veggie tempura, kale chips, pickled root veggies, yam fries, plus crepes, several sliders and sausages, spaetzle, gnocchi, mac & cheese (ask for spicy!)

Drink Specials 2
$3.50 local brews; $4.00 gluten-free or German pints; $5.00 wine

Atmosphere 3
Back in the day, this was il Piatto. Same owners, different concept. Decor-wise, the revamped interior incorporates Alpine Inn elements with a mid-century modern cocktail swank. Simple and cozy charm with some hipster kitsch.

Why I Really Like It
Caring attention to offering healthy food options, occasional live music (plus frequent bands next door at the Jade Lounge), and awesome brunch!

Southpark

Downtown (West) Map
901 SW Salmon
(503) 326-1300
www.southparkseafood.com

Happy Hours
3:00–6:00pm and 10:00pm-close Daily

Food Deals 3
$5.00
A better-than-ever menu changes often, but you'll find food to match your mood with things like roasted veggies, peppers, Brussels sprouts, glazed turnips, carrots, salads, pizza, clam chowder, oysters, burger, and boards.

Drink Specials 3
$5.00 drafts; $5.00 red, white or sparklings
$5.00 sangria; $5.00 wells

Atmosphere 3
Southpark has been a perennial favorite of many a Portlander, myself included. It just works on so many levels. Be aware that it's more of a bar than a romantic wine-date place and that it can get crowded. Outstanding wine selection.

Why I Really Like It
One of the original besties. Everyone I've ever had a conversation with about this place has said they love it. And they've finally really upped their Happy Hour offerings!

SAT-SUN

St. Jack

NW/Nob Hill Map
1610 NW 23rd Ave
(503) 360-1281
www.stjackpdx.com

Happy Hours
4:00-6:00pm and 10:00pm-close Daily

Food Deals 3
$3.00–$9.00
French bistro hors d'oeuvres like poutine, farm fresh salads, gruyére burger, crispy pork rinds, cheeses, mussels; or for the brave, fried tripe!

Drink Specials 2
$4.00 select beers; $5.00-$7.00 wines
$7.00-$9.00 choice of three cocktails

Atmosphere 3
They moved a couple years ago from their location at SE Clinton & 20th. Interior is quite similar with whites and creams against black woods and chalkboard menus, but more contemporary than vintage Parisian. Big and open corner-lot bistro with large central bar and giant windows to the street, with restaurant side next door.

Why I Really Like It
When Paris is just a bit too far away, you can catch a piece of fancy French food and fun.

The Station

Alberta Map
2703 NE Alberta
(503) 284-4491
www.stationpdx.com

Happy Hours
4:00–6:30pm Daily; ★All night Tuesday

Food Deals 3
$4.50–$7.75
Sports bar pub fare with an international spin: kung pao wings, beer cheese mac, pork nachos, Korean tacos, soup, taquitos, tots, sweet potato skins, hoisin ginger green beans.

Drink Specials 2
$1.00 off domestics; $5.00 wine; $7.00 mules

Atmosphere 3
Sported-up from recent years as Siam Society. Super-high ceilings with rough cement walls and a towering, illuminated, mirrored wall of booze. A popular place, so it can be a bit loud, but a wonderful back beer garden awaits! Dog friendly too, for our four-legged friends.

Why I Really Like It
Architecturally, this former Electric Company building looks so cool both outside and in! And though it's not on the HH menu, they got me addicted to their grilled calamari! Cool bar.

Streetcar Bistro & Taproom

Pearl Map
1101 NW Northrup
(503) 227-2988
www.streetcarbistro.com

Happy Hours
3:00-6:00pm /10:00pm-mid Mon-Sat
★All day Sunday

Food Deals 3
$3.00-$7.00
About 10 items of all sorts that vary seasonally: salads, soup, BBQ pork sandwich, mac & cheese, bacon-wrapped dates, deelish burgers.

Drink Specials 3
$4.00 daily draft; $6.00 wine
$6.00-$8.00 specialty cocktails

Atmosphere 3
Sleek modern look with muted white pine woods, white leather boxy chairs, and a big bar with a brilliant wall of beautiful, illuminated taps. Nice lounge area with couches and fireplace.

Why I Really Like It
It's quite a heavenly beer place hosting 30 rotating craft beer taps with emphasis on NW brews.
FYI – big selection of scotch and whiskeys.
Nice place to hang out and lots of live music too.

SAT-SUN

Sunshine Tavern

Southeast Map
3111 SE Division
(503) 688-1750
www.sunshinepdx.com

Happy Hours
5:00-6:00pm and 10:00-11:00pm Tues-Sun

Food Deals 3
$1.50–$6.00
Comfort/bar food with a NW-gourmet twist: pickled eggs, olives, cheese fries with pork and gravy, romaine salad, crispy oysters, ham panini, corn dog, candied hazelnuts, and pasta.

Drink Specials 3
$4.00 draft beer; $5.00 house wines
$6.00 slushy margarita
$5.00 bartender's choice cocktail

Atmosphere 3
Rain or shine, the sky-high windows let in lots of light, and the wood walls and booths warm the place up. After the sun sets, it takes on a totally different, more intimate glow, perfect for indulging those late-night munchie cravings.

Why I Really Like It
A second, much more casual place from Chef Jenn Louis of Lincoln Restaurant on WIlliams!

Swank & Swine

North/NE Map
808 SW Taylor
(503) 943-5844
www.swankandswine.com

Happy Hours
3:30-6:30pm Daily

Food Deals 3
$1.50-$8.00
Bar basics, but better: Burgers, deviled eggs, calamari, shrimp, Caesar, spuds, ribs, rinds, wings.

Drink Specials 3
$4.00 drafts; $6.00 wine; $6.00 wells & cocktails

Atmosphere 3
The cool and swanky "Swine" side is located in the old Dragonfish space in the Paramount Hotel. Well-designed concept incarnating a prohibition-style moonshine and whiskey bar. Walls covered in reclaimed woods with open space, lounge areas, and covetable wall of whiskey lockers.

Why I Really Like It
Cool space! But thankfully not overly porked out food-wise, despite the name.

Swift & Union

North/NE Map
8103 N Denver Ave.
(503) 206-4281
www.swiftandunion.com

Happy Hours
4:00-6:00pm Mon-Fri

Food Deals 3 $2.00-$6.00
Nice mix of cafe food that keeps up with the changing seasons: soup, salad, fish & chips, union burger, beef tips, pumpkin fritters, pretzel.

Drink Specials 3
$3.75 drafts; $5.00 wine; $5.00 rotating cocktail

Atmosphere 3
Not taught in Design School, their soon-to-be-trending "butcher shop chic" look establishes this newly-beloved neighborhood bar as *the* prominent hot spot in the 'hood. Open space split between back bar and dining room, with butcher block tables, random cow heads, white tiled walls and some very creative lights.

Why I Really Like It
Holy cow! Kenton has its first restaurant that has made an appearance in my book, and I love what they've done with the place! I'll be back, and probably often. Named after 1907 Swift Meat Packing and Union Meat merger.

Tabla

Lloyd Center-ish Map
200 NE 28th Ave
(503) 238-3777
www.tablapastaevino.com

Happy Hours
5:00–6:00pm Tues-Sat

Food Deals 3
$2.50–$7.50
One of the Northwest's best offers Happy Hour with half-off all pastas (large or smaller dinners), plus a few nibble plates like Steve's cheese or charcuterie, crostini. I forget how delicious it is!

Drink Specials 3
$3.00 drafts; $5.00 house wines; $12 half carafe
$5.00 wells; $5.00 Negroni

Atmosphere 3
Simple and modern decor with banquette seating, Fresh flowers on tables and at windows, and pleasant dinner music. Happy Hour is at bar only Fri-Sat. Seasonal sidewalk seating.

Why I Really Like It
A consistently highly-rated, but way-too-under-the-radar place. Great food and wine at such a deal at Happy Hour! A renewed fave every time I go.

Tapalaya

Lloyd Center-ish Map
28 NE 28th Ave
(503) 232-6652
www.tapalaya.com

Happy Hours
4:00–6:00pm Daily

Food Deals 3
$3.00–$5.00
Tapas/bites of New Orleans menu just about perfect for getting one of everything to share, like the Tapalaya trio (sampler changes daily), skewers, bahn mi, wings, or Mississippi caviar.

Drink Specials 3
$5.00 red, white, or rosé wine
$3.00 martinis and $4.00 hurricanes
$5.00 signature cocktail specials

Atmosphere 3
Laissez les bon temps rouler! Not wild, but fun; more cozy and cute; neighborhoody and nice. Live music Tues & Thur 6-9pm – check calendar.

Why I Really Like It
I love their spicy chips! I love their Mississippi caviar! And I REALLY love their jambalaya! And I love that serving sizes are just a tad smaller so I can enjoy a big variety all in one sitting :-)

SAT-SUN

Tasty n Alder

Downtown (West) Map
580 SW 12th Ave.
(503) 621-9251
www.tastyntasty.com

Happy Hours 2:00–5:30pm Daily

Food Deals 3
$1.00–$9.00
A bit different menu than their northside original, Tasty n Sons. Same owners of Toro Bravo. Hush puppies, paté or cheese boards, fried chicken, chili dog, egg dishes, fries, salad, phenomenal steak sandwich. All so very tasty!

Drink Specials 3
$2.00 mini-mugs (3); $7.00 wines
$7.00 tasty cocktail specials

Atmosphere 3
Trendy Northwest stylings much like the other Tasty. Reclaimed woods, open ceiling rafters and visable ducts, silver metal accents and lights, wood benches and white chairs.

Why I Really Like It
The steak sandwich! And 2:00pm start time. This place gets continual rave reviews. Same with the other **Tasty n'Sons** (3808 NE Williams), but that location is just way too loud for me to rave about. It's packed and popular though!

Tavern on Kruse

Lake Oswego
4835 Meadows Rd #133
(503) 303-5280
www.tavernonkruse.com

Happy Hours
4:00-6:00pm Mon–Fri

Food Deals 3
$4.00-$8.00
Unique and delicious delights that change often, and there's lots of them! Autumn may bring things like an apple & butternut squash soup, red chili chicken tacos with habenero crema, or a bacon, pear, and fontina flatbread. Salads, ceviche, fries, dips, and a dessert of perfection.

Drink Specials 3
$4.75 beer/cider; $7.00 wine; $1.00 off cocktails

Atmosphere 3
Stunning! It's called Tavern, but in a Tavern on the Green kind of way. In the far NE corner of Kruse Village Shopping Center is a lovely piazza with a fountain and container garden. Inside, huge windows with tiered glass shelving showcases glowing, colorful bottles. Contemporary, classy and cosmopolitan.

New this Year/First Impressions
Visually, it's a stunner! New York style in the 'burbs. Relaxing, with top-notch food.

SAT / ALL SUN

Thai Bloom

NW Location
333 NW 23rd Ave.; (503) 243-7557
Beaverton Location
3800 SW Cedar Hills; (503) 644-8010
www.thaibloomrestaurant.com

New!

GOLDEN TICKET!

Happy Hours
4:00-6:00pm Daily; ★Noon-9:00pm Sun
8:00-9:00pm Mon-Thur; 9:00-10:00pm Fri-Sat

Food Deals 3+ $2.99-$6.99
Insanely huge menu with over 20 choices and exceptionally delicious food! Nice mix of classics and also some more unusual items. Setting a high bar for Thai HH with a bit of everything!

Drink Specials 3
$4.00 beer; $5.00 wine; $1.00 off wells
$5.99 specialty cocktails

Atmosphere 2
<u>Northwest</u> – Second location near but not in the old Typhoon, where many of their cooks hail from. Modern, black & white with specs of red.
<u>Beaverton</u> – Black & white, modern lighting, big granite square bar surrounded by tables. Patio.

New this Year/First Impressions
I've LOVED the one in Beaverton, and am very happy that this new location opened up, too. So many choices and such good, high-quality Thai food at amazingly low prices!

SAT / ALL SUN

Thirst Bistro

Willamette River
0315 SW Montgomery
(503) 295-2747
www.thirstbistro.com

~ 2016 ~
TOP 10
Superstar

GOLDEN TICKET!

Happy Hours
3:00–6:00pm Tues–Sun (All day Sun)

Food Deals 3
$2.00–$6.00
Delicious nibbles perfect with wine (plan and pair your choices): hot crab dip, baked brie, stuffed and wrapped dates, chili, salads and soups. Plus sharable charcuterie and cheese plates, and flat iron steak with mashed potatoes ($9.00).

Drink Specials 3
$3.00 beer; $5.00 select wine (try the $9.00 flight)
$5.50 cocktail of the day

Atmosphere 3
Right on RiverPlace Esplanade with huge windows and sidewalk seating for people- and river-gazing; lovely lounge area with comfy couch and fireplace. A truly enjoyable wine bar, now with a separate NW wine tasting room.

Why I Really Like It
Excellent food, views, ambiance and wine! What's not to love?! A true DON'T MISS! Ahh... to sip a wine flight or two in the summer sun...

Three Degrees

SAT-SUN

Willamette River
1510 SW Harbor Way (RiverPlace)
(503) 295-6166
www.threedegreesrestaurant.com

Happy Hours
4:00–6:00pm Daily

Food Deals 3
$3.00–$6.00
They got their groove back with a new chef and a well-developed menu that changes seasonally: Mixed greens, chorizo, or roasted beet salads, bacon-wrapped oysters, crab deviled eggs, crispy oyster sliders with brie, hamachi, and more.

Drink Specials 3
$4.00 drafts; $4.00 red or white wine
$5.00 wells; $5.00 cocktail of the day

Atmosphere 3
Romantic upscale perfection; river view with lots of windows, cushy seats, and a cozy fireplace. Summer weather treats us to their fun outdoor deck. Free valet parking (with tip)!

Why I Really Like It
This riverfront area is just so lovely! They've done a slight remodel and brought up their food level too. This place has changed with the tides, but I think they are once again standing on solid ground.

Touché

Pearl Map
1425 NW Glisan; (503) 221-1150
www.touchepdx.com

Happy Hours
4:00-6:30pm and 10:00pm–close Daily
(11:00pm Fri-Sat)
★All day Sunday (4:00pm–close)

Food Deals 3
$3.50–$7.00
Crazy-huge menu and big servings! Four kinds of gyros (chicken, lamb, falafel, or veggie), wood-fired pizza, salads, Mediterranean platter, spaghetti bolognese, lasagna, burger with fries, steamed clams, dips/spreads, tiramisu, and more!

Drink Specials 3
$1.00 off drafts; $4.00 wells; $5.00 wines

Atmosphere 3
Happy Hour anywhere in the gorgeous restaurant downstairs, upstairs in the semi-stately pool hall, or out on the wonderful new patio(s)! Grand staircase entrance and six nice, full-size tables. Great for both stylish pool boys and true sharks.

Why I Really Like It
Tons of choices and they are the size of real meals, but don't cost much at all! It's like three places in one depending if you sit in the restaurant, out on the deck, or up in the pool room.

SAT / ALL SUN

Trader Vic's

Pearl Map
1203 NW Glisan; (503) 467-2277
www.tradervicspdx.com

GOLDEN TICKET!

Happy Hours
3:00–6:00pm Daily;10:00pm-close Fri-Sat
★All day Sunday (11:00am–close)

Food Deals 3 $4.00-$7.00
Twelve exceptionally delicious tiki treats! Glazed chicken wings, Korean beef tacos, calamari, fries, char sui pork, sliders, coconut shrimp, stir-fried chicken in lettuce cups, wontons, salad, beans.

Drink Specials 3
$4.00 drafts; $5.00 red or white house wines
$6.00 mai tais and signature tropical cocktails

Atmosphere 3+
A Polynesian piece of paradise in the Pearl! Refined, tropical, tiki elegance mixed with fun, fascination, and fire. It's fully enchanting and magical! Thatched ceilings and walls, bamboo and carved wooden masks everywhere, and a social, central tiki bar with themed cocktail-ware. Full walls of windows open to the street.

Why I Really Like It
It gives you the feeling of a tropical vacation all over, via decor, food, and when you're sipping a drink from one of their signature crazy mugs! A total fave and Happy Hour of the Year 2014.

Uchu Sushi

NE/Mississippi Map
3940 N Mississippi
(503) 281-8248
www.uchusushi.com

Happy Hours
2:00-6:00pm Daily; 12:00pm-close Mon–Wed ★
9:00pm-close Thur-Sat

Food Deals 3
$4.00–$5.00
Wow! Delightful and very extensive menu offers 13 small plates and 14 sushi rolls. Baked mussels, egg rolls, wings, poppers, gyoza, calamari, yakitori, several salads, and the full array of classic sushi rolls. $6.50-$8.00 dinner bowls too.

Drink Specials 3
$1.00 off all beer, wine, and sakes
$3.00 wells; $2.00 off all cocktails

Atmosphere 2
Officially known as Uchu Sushi & Fried Chicken. Casual, Portland-style, industrial chic. Cement floors, long front bar, wood tables and roll top garage doors/window. Iconic, ironic, giant fish tanks!

Why I Really Like It
Giant menu and low prices on tasty food. Not fancy, but still a fave.

SAT

Uptown Billiards Club

NW/Nob Hill Map
120 NW 23rd Ave.
(503) 226-6909
www.uptownbilliards.com

A PERFECT 10
10 YEARS
– and counting –

GOLDEN TICKET!

Happy Hours
4:00–6:00pm Tues–Sat

Food Deals 3
About a dozen, pretty much half-price items: Seasonal selections: pork belly sliders, nachos, arancini, deviled eggs, mini beef wellington or a bacon, pear, and fontina pizza.

Drink Specials 3
$4.00 drafts; $5.00-$6.00 wines
$1.00 off wells; $5.50–$7.00 cocktails

Atmosphere 3
Totally different in the pool hall classification with its upscale class and elegence. There's a nice, big room for playing pool, a gorgeous wooden bar, a small dining room and a private, tucked-away billiards room.

Why I Really Like It
Huge and awesome Happy Hour yes, but if you want one of the best dining experiences ever, try their five-course pairing menu. W-O-W!!! Also, check out their new brother restaurant, Tavern on Kruse in Lake Oswego (p.236).

SAT-SUN

Urban Farmer

Downtown (East) Map
525 SW Morrison
(503) 222-4900
www.urbanfarmerrestaurant.com

Happy Hours
3:00–6:00pm/10:00pm–close Daily (11pm Fri-Sat)

Food Deals 3 $2.00–$8.00
Farm-fresh NW delights and seasonal updates, and changing options from the earth, ocean and range: chicken pops, bangers & mash, sliders, lobster salad roll, skewers, oysters, meatballs, deviled eggs, and soup (but sadly, no salads).

Drink Specials 3
$5.00 drafts; $6.00 house wines
$5.00 cocktail of the day

Atmosphere 3+
Absolutely stunning! The number one decor award winner! Truly a Portland stand-out in the giant, cavernous atrium of the Hotel Nines with cozy, mini-atrium seating areas. Ultra-modern style with subtle rustic touches. Coolest at night!

Why I Really Like It
I step in and I want to open an office there to hang out all day in the open luxury of it all! It's a really cool space, and Departure (which is another ultimate fave) is just a few floors up!

SAT-SUN

Verde Cucina

Pearl Map
524 NW 14th Ave.
(503) 894-9321
www.verdecocinamarket.com
plus:
Hillsdale: 6446 SW Capitol Hwy; (503) 384-2327
NEW! Sylvan Highlands: 5515 SW Canyon Ct; (503) 297-5568

Happy Hours 3:30–5:00pm Daily

Food Deals 3 $3.00-$7.00
Such good food here! Now three locations with slight variations in menus: ceviche, tacos, Guac & tortillas, fundido, salad, roasted veggies.

Drink Specials 3
$1.00 off beer; $5.00 wine; $5.00 sangritas
$6.00 Margaritas or palomas

Atmosphere 2
Formerly Kin and before that Holden's. Simple, small space with little adornment. Open, central bar area, roll-up garage doors, orange walls, wood floors, and black metal chairs.

Why I Really Like It
It's all about the food here! Per their website, "Northwest farm-to-fork ingredients with a Mexican flair." Local seasonal focus in the hands of excellent chefs = BUENO!

Via Delizia

SAT-SUN

Pearl Map
1105 NW Marshall
(503) 225-9300
www.viadelizia.com

Happy Hours
3:00–6:00pm Daily

Food Deals 3
$4.00–$6.00
Good portions and great food! Bruschetta, salads, ravioli, spaghetti alla bolognese, pork panini, and several flatbreads (steak, chicken or caprese). Be sure to save room for the gelato!

Drink Specials 0
Sadly, no drink deals, but low prices at all times

Atmosphere
A giant tree dominates overhead and creates a pleasant patio piazza scene inside. Hanging lights, stone walls, an arched wooden doorway, and shutters on windows all conspire to help transport you to Italy. Cozy little Italian street-side café!

Why I Really Like It
It's just a really cute place with great value on great food and super-cutest at night. Warning – the gelato is deliriously addicting!

Victoria

Northeast (Near Mississippi)
4835 N Albina
No phone
www.victoriapdx.com

Happy Hours
3:00-6:00pm Daily

Food Deals 2 $2.00-$7.00
Short, simple menu with five items: Pulled pork sandwich, daily vegan po' boy, black eyed pea fritters, pickles, and a pimento mac & cheese that many are loving, especially vegans.

Drink Specials 2
$4.00 beer; $6.00 Victoria Mules
$5.00 house wines; $4.00 wells, $5.00 punch

Atmosphere 2
This used to be <u>Trebol</u> a few years ago. They've revamped the space and opened it all up, including the now-much-larger outdoor patio. The front half is part contemporary cocktail bar and part working man tavern mixed with pretty dashes of Victorian charm. The back half is pretty barren, with big garage doors open to the outside. Giant white shelves dominate, and are beautifully illuminated and super-stocked. Bar service only.

New this Year/First Impressions
The jury is still out on this one. I prefer to be waited on, and I like big menus with more options.

Wild Abandon

Southeast Map
2411 SE Belmont
(503) 232-4458
www.wildabandonrestaurant.com

Happy Hours
4:30–6:30pm Mon, Wed–Fri

Food Deals 3
$1.00-$8.00
Choose from about 15 gourmet specialties including shrimp or chicken with peppers over polenta, extra-delicious portobello sandwich(!), soup, burger, several salads, mac & cheese, BBQ pork sandwich, goat cheese torta, or fries.

Drink Specials 3
$4.00 drafts; $5.00 wine; $5.00 well drinks
$5.00–$6.00 big array of cocktails

Atmosphere 3
A funky little "Love Shack" as viewed from the street; things change inside with cozy, dimly lit dining. Colorful, glass hanging lamps and a mishmash of framed prints add to the garage-sale-chic, retro look. Wonderful garden patio in back!

Why I Really Like It
Wild Abandon is a big go-to place for me. It's just kind of low-key and casual, but the Happy Hour here hits it right everytime. Great food and prices at dinner and weekend brunch too!

SAT-SUN

XV (15)

Old Town Map
15 SW 2nd Ave.
(503) 790-9090
www.barfifteen.com

Happy Hours
4:00–7:00pm Daily and 9:00pm-mid Sat-Thur

Food Deals 3
$2.00–$4.50
Half off a big selection of good food! Who knew?! Yellow curry fried rice with zucchini and squash, roasted red pepper quesadilla, yam or seasoned fries with dipping sauces, pork or beef sliders, three kinds of tacos, spinach and tomato or Cajun mac & cheese; plus house, Caesar or roasted beet salads. Prized price and taste mix!

Drink Specials 2
$1.00 PBRs; $3.00 drafts
$4.00 wells; $6.00 signature cocktails

Atmosphere 2
Dark, simple, *very* casual bar area, but cool-candlelit lounge with couches in back room. Not necessarily recommended late-night.

Why I Really Like It
NOT fancy at all, but thought I'd throw at least one really good borderline dive bar in the mix! I'm solely looking at Happy Hour here – tasty, substantial, some healthy picks, and cheap!

Zoiglhaus Brewing Co.

Southeast (off Map)
5716 SE 92nd Ave.
(971) 339-2374
www.zoiglhaus.com

Happy Hours
3:00-5:30pm and 9:00pm-close Daily

Food Deals 2
$3.00-$5.00
German beer hall grub: Flammkuchen of the day (name literally means "flaming pie/tart/cake" i.e. flatbread), currywurst, turkey meatballs, burger, pretzel, hummus, fries, or a pickled platter.

Drink Specials 2 $1.00 off haus-made pints

Atmosphere 3
The Lents neighbors are rejoicing over this fine new addition to the 'hood! Two large dining rooms on each side, with a big social bar in the middle section. Stark at this point, but nice, with navy and white walls and a growing collection of German beer signs. Zoigl is a variety of beer brewed in eastern Bavaria, and the beer brewed here is very impressive.

New this Year/First Impressions
I LOVE the beer here, and hope to find it on taps all throughout the city soon!

Been there – Done that!

Restaurant Name	Notes/Memories/People

Yes! I've been!

First, The Top 10s:

- ☐ Altabira
- ☐ Amalfi's
- ☐ Bellino
- ☐ Lechon
- ☐ Mama Mia Trattoria
- ☐ McCormick & Schmick's
- ☐ North 45
- ☐ Ruth's Chris
- ☐ Seres
- ☐ Thirst Bistro

- ☐ 23 Hoyt
- ☐ Altabira
- ☐ Amalfi's
- ☐ Aquariva
- ☐ Aviary
- ☐ Bacchus
- ☐ Bamboo Sushi
- ☐ Bartini
- ☐ Barlow
- ☐ Bazi Bierbrasserie

Been there – Done that!

Restaurant Name	Notes
☐ Bellino	_____
☐ Benson	_____
☐ Bent Brick	_____
☐ Bit House Saloon	_____
☐ Bluehour	_____
☐ Brix	_____
☐ Cafe Castagna	_____
☐ Cafe Nell	_____
☐ Casa del Matador	_____
☐ Ciao Vito	_____
☐ Cibo	_____
☐ Clarklewis	_____
☐ Cellar 55	_____
☐ Chez Machin	_____
☐ Circa 33	_____
☐ Clyde Common	_____
☐ DarSalam	_____
☐ Departure	_____
☐ Dragonwell	_____
☐ Driftwood Room	_____
☐ East India Company	_____
☐ Ecliptic Brewing	_____
☐ El Gaucho	_____
☐ Elini's Philoxenia	_____

Been there – Done that!

Restaurant Name	Notes
☐ Elephant's Deli	_____
☐ Epif	_____
☐ Equinox	_____
☐ Farm Café	_____
☐ The Fields	_____
☐ Firehouse	_____
☐ Gold Dust Meridian	_____
☐ Grant House	_____
☐ High Noon	_____
☐ Hokusei Sushi	_____
☐ Hop City Tavern	_____
☐ Iconic	_____
☐ Imperial	_____
☐ Interurban	_____
☐ Irving Street Kitchen	_____
☐ Island Cafe	_____
☐ Jake's Famous	_____
☐ Jake's Grill	_____
☐ Jantzen Beach Bar	_____
☐ Karam	_____
☐ La Calaca Comelona	_____
☐ Lapellah	_____
☐ Las Primas	_____
☐ Lechon	_____

Been there – Done that!

Restaurant Name	**Notes**
☐ Levant	_____
☐ Lincoln	_____
☐ Mama Mia Trattoria	_____
☐ Manzana Grill	_____
☐ Marmo	_____
☐ Masu Sushi	_____
☐ McCormick & Schmick's	_____
☐ Meriwether's	_____
☐ Mother's	_____
☐ Muselet	_____
☐ Nel Centro	_____
☐ Night Light	_____
☐ Noble Rot	_____
☐ Noho's	_____
☐ North 45	_____
☐ North Light	_____
☐ Nostrana	_____
☐ Oba	_____
☐ Oven & Shaker	_____
☐ Paadee	_____
☐ Paddy's	_____
☐ Paley's Place	_____
☐ Pambiche	_____
☐ Papa Hayden	_____

Been there – Done that!

Restaurant Name	Notes
☐ Park Kitchen	
☐ Peddler & The Pen	
☐ Petisco	
☐ Piattino	
☐ Pine Shed Ribs	
☐ Pink Rose	
☐ Portland City Grill	
☐ Portland Penny Diner	
☐ Portland Prime	
☐ Pour Wine Bar	
☐ Produce Row Cafe	
☐ Ringside Glendoveer	
☐ Ringside Fish House	
☐ Riverview	
☐ Ruth's Chris	
☐ Saké	
☐ Salty's	
☐ Salvador Molly's	
☐ Sapphire Hotel	
☐ Saucebox	
☐ Seres	
☐ Serratto	
☐ Slide Inn	
☐ Southpark	

Been there – Done that!

Restaurant Name	Notes
☐ St. Jack	
☐ The Station	
☐ Streetcar Bistro	
☐ Sunshine Tavern	
☐ Swank & Swine	
☐ Swift & Union	
☐ Tabla	
☐ Tapalaya	
☐ Tasty & Alder	
☐ Tavern on Kruse	
☐ Thai Bloom	
☐ Thirst Bistro	
☐ Three Degrees	
☐ Touche	
☐ Trader Vic's	
☐ Uchu Sushi	
☐ Uptown Billiards	
☐ Urban Farmer	
☐ Verde Cucina	
☐ Via Delizia	
☐ Victoria	
☐ Wild Abandon	
☐ XV	
☐ Zoiglhaus Brewery	